A Bit of F

Stephen Fry and Hugh Laurie are both
writers, comedians, and actors. Stephen Fry
wrote the script of the musical *Me and My Girl*.
He regularly appears on television and radio
and he writes a weekly column for the *Daily
Telegraph*. Hugh Laurie has recently starred in
Ben Elton's play *Gasping* in the West End. Fry
and Laurie both appeared regularly in
Blackadder with Rowan Atkinson and they have
starred in two series of *A Bit of Fry and Laurie*.
They are currently working on a second series
of *Jeeves and Wooster*.

STEPHEN FRY and HUGH LAURIE

A Bit of
Fry and Laurie

Mandarin

A Mandarin Paperback

A BIT OF FRY AND LAURIE

First published in Great Britain 1990
Reprinted 1990 (twice)
by Mandarin Paperbacks
Michelin House, 81 Fulham Road, London SW3 6RB

Mandarin is an imprint of the Octopus Publishing Group

Copyright © 1990 by Stephen Fry and Hugh Laurie

A CIP catalogue record for this title
is available from the British Library
ISBN 0 7493 0705 6

Stills from A BIT OF FRY AND LAURIE
copyright © 1990 *Radio Times*
Photograph of Stephen Fry and Hugh Laurie
copyright © 1990 by Mike Prior

Printed and bound in Great Britain
by Cox & Wyman Ltd, Reading

Caution
All rights whatsoever in these sketches are strictly reserved
and applications for permission to perform them in whole or
in part must be made in advance, before rehearsals begin,
to David Higham Associates Ltd, 5–8 Lower John Street,
Golden Square, London W1R 4HA

To Bobby Robson

Thanks to Roger Ordish, for managing to produce the show in between episodes of 'Sir James Savile Will Bring His Influence to Bear in Arranging Matters to Your Satisfaction'; to Uri Geller for being so laughable; and to the waiter for finding Stephen's glasses.

Contents

Introduction

Stephen   Well Hugh, here's the book.

Hugh   Absolutely.

Stephen   Well put. *(Slight pause)* So, any advice for someone who's just picked this book up, say, in one of the many fresh, clean High Street bookshops that stock this important new work and is considering, if not making a purchase, then at least slipping it down his or her trouser or trousers?

Hugh   Well Stephen, I'd like firstly to congratulate the potential thief on his or her good taste or tastes, but I'd like to follow up that congratulation quite smartly with a caveat or warning.

Hugh breaks off and looks over Stephen's shoulder or shoulders. There is a longish pause.

Stephen   Yes. I'm busy wondering what the nature of that caveat or warning might be, Hugh.

Hugh   *(Jerking back)* I'm sorry, I thought I saw something dark, vivid and unpleasant.

Stephen   It must have been your imagination.

Hugh   Probably. No, the caveat, rejoinder, admonishment or warning I would make to the potential thief of this book is this. No matter who you are, no matter what your name is, no matter how far away you run, no matter how you try to disguise yourself with towels and the cunning application of coloured yoghurts, no matter what lengths you go to, no matter how well you protect yourself, we will seek you out and destroy you.

Stephen   Eventually.

Hugh	We will destroy you eventually. And when we do . . .
Stephen	Well . . .
Hugh	Exactly.
Stephen	So. Just remember. You can run, but you can't hop.
Hugh	We'll be there. Across the street. In dark glasses.
Stephen	Arms folded.
Hugh	Watching.
Stephen	In silent reproach.
Hugh	So just you trot over to the desk and pay the nice lady cash money for this book.
Stephen	Apart from anything else, you'll find that if you don't none of the jokes will be at all funny.
Hugh	That's right. Every sketch will have a punchline limper than . . .
Stephen	Limper than . . .
Hugh	Limper than a very limp thing that's especially limp today.
Stephen	Exactly. But hey! That's the heavy part over with. Let's tell the average honest and surprisingly pretty punter a little about the genesis of this book, shall we Hugh?
Hugh	This book doesn't have a genesis, Stephen. You're thinking of the bible.
Stephen	Ha, what a very nearly laughable misunderstanding, Hugh. I meant 'genesis' in the sense of 'beginning or inception'.
Hugh	*(Wiping his eyes with laughter)* Oh! I see! And *I* thought . . .
Stephen	*(Falling about)* Dear oh dear.

They pick themselves up off the floor at length.

No, this book came about as a result, didn't it Hugh, of enormous commercial pressure to make the written texts of *A Bit of Fry And Laurie* available to the public at large.

Hugh   When you say 'enormous commercial pressure' you mean . . . ?

Stephen   I mean some drunken overpaid publishing executive thought it might be a good way of staving off their eventual dismissal.

Hugh   Right.

Stephen   We wrote these sketches over a period of . . . what, Hugh?

Hugh   Over a period of time, if I remember rightly.

Stephen   Over a period of months between June and December 1987.

Hugh   When the world was young and everything seemed slightly frilly.

Stephen   Why did we write these sketches, you may ask?

Hugh   Well, let me turn that question round and say 'Why did we sketch these writes, you may ask?'

Stephen   Let me turn *that* question round and say 'Why did we write these sketches, you ask may?'

Hugh   Because they were there.

Stephen   No, Hugh, because they *weren't* there. That's the whole point. Amazingly, no-one had written those sketches before.

Hugh   The Pythons had written something pretty similar though hadn't they?

Stephen looks uncomfortable.

Stephen	*(Through clenched teeth)* Shut *up*, Hugh.
Hugh	Sorry.
Stephen	No, as we say these sketches are the original children of our minds.
Hugh	They're our babies.
Stephen	In a sense, yes. In a wholly unacceptable sense.
Hugh	Yes, because that's not to imply that we literally went to bed together, introduced various fleshy nozzles into each other's warm places and then gave birth to a pile of paper covered in amusing sketch material, is it Stephen?
Stephen	Hugh.
Hugh	Yes?
Stephen	Shut your bleeding neck for a moment will you?
Hugh	Right-o.
Stephen	These sketches are for your perusalment and enjoyage to do with what you will.
Hugh	Within certain rather exciting legal parameters.
Stephen	That's right. We ought to mention that you can't actually *perform* these sketches in public to a fee-paying audience.
Hugh	Though why anyone should want to perform these sketches in public beats me with a wet napkin.
Stephen	Oh I don't know Hugh.
Hugh	Don't you?
Stephen	No.
Hugh	Oh.
Stephen	Imagine your plane has been hijacked by a gang of terrorists and their leader, a rather desperate character called Miguel, threatens to shoot all

4

the passengers unless someone can perform the
'Haircut' sketch in the Club Class lavatory.

Hugh   Of course you're right. How silly of me.

Stephen   Well in those circumstances it would be quite
illegal for you to accede to his wishes.

Hugh   Quite right. We do not deal with terrorists.

Stephen   All we can suggest is that you volunteer to write
a sketch very similar to 'Haircut', and that you'll
promise to have it finished and in rehearsal by the
time you reach Libyan air space.

Hugh   Yes. Just remember that Miguel's bark is much
worse that his bite.

Stephen   And he cannot bear split infinitives.

Hugh   So that's got that out of the way. Anything else
that the discerning consumer need know in order
to extract maximum reading pleasure from these
pages, Stephen?

Stephen   Oh just the basics. Consult your GP, wipe down
all surfaces with a damp dry cloth, and do not go
to sleep with your head on a railway line.

Hugh   Sound advice. Although Stephen, isn't there
one vital step you should take before consulting
your GP?

Stephen   Absolutely, Hugh. Before consulting your GP,
please please please consult your GP.

Hugh   For those of you reading in black and white,
Stephen put a lot of emphasis on that third
'please'.

Stephen   Yes. Although I hope I didn't completely neglect
the first two.

Hugh   Of course not.

Stephen   Once you've taken those basic, common sense

5

measures, it's just a question of relaxing, kicking off your shoes, slipping into a loose-fitting kimono and going over to the cash desk to buy this book.

Hugh   Although if you've read this far without buying it, we can only assume that it's raining pretty heavily outside.

Stephen Looks as if it's brightening a bit over there . . .

Hugh   D'you know, you may be right . . .

Spies One

Hugh comes into the office. Stephen is sitting behind a desk.

Hugh   Hello, Control.

Stephen   Oh. Hello there, Murchison. How are you today?

Hugh   Very well indeed as a matter of fact, Control.

Stephen   That's good.

Hugh   Yes.

Faintly uncomfortable pause.

Stephen   So. Anyway. What can I 'do you for'?!

Hugh   Well. This just came through flash from Berlin, sir. I thought perhaps you might like to take a look at it.

Stephen   Flash from Berlin, eh? Well I better had. We've got quite a few valuable agents in Berlin, haven't we? It might be something quite urgent, I expect.

Hugh   Yes.

Stephen   *(Reading)* I see Valerie has decoded it for me. That's kind of her. Saves me quite a bit of extra work. I must remember to thank her.

Hugh   That would certainly be a nice gesture, sir.

Stephen   Well, much as I expected. I don't know if you had an opportunity to look through it, Tony, before thoughtfully bringing it into me, but it is quite an urgent message from Firefly, our network head in Berlin.

Hugh	Yes, I had time just to glance at the codename as I came in. Firefly is under deep cover. Has something quite important happened to make him break it like this?
Stephen	Well that was the first thought that crossed my mind, Tony, certainly. It looks as if his network has been penetrated by an enemy agent.
Hugh	Oh no.
Stephen	Yes, I'm afraid so. All his men have been arrested. Glow-worm was shot attempting to cross over into the west and Firefly himself is hiding up somewhere at a safehouse in the east.
Hugh	So the whole network has been blown?
Stephen	That's right. It's a thundering nuisance.
Hugh	It certainly is. Thundering.
Stephen	I'm severely vexed, I don't mind telling you.
Hugh	I expect a coffee would come in welcome then.
Stephen	Well it certainly couldn't hurt, could it?
Hugh	No. Not just one. I'll get Valerie onto it.
Stephen	Thank you so much, Tony.
Hugh	You're very welcome.

Makes to go. Turns from the door.

	Let's hope it's not going to turn out to be one of those days, eh, Control? Like Thursday.
Stephen	Oh! That's all we need! I don't know! See you later then, Tony.
Hugh	Alright.

8

Censored

Stephen   Ladies and gentlemen, we were going to do a sketch for you . . .

Hugh   But we're not now.

Stephen   No, we're not going to do it for you, now.

Hugh   Or ever.

Stephen   Or probably ever. Unless this country radically changes direction.

Hugh   Looks unlikely.

Stephen   Which does indeed look unlikely. The reason we're not going to do this sketch is that it contains a great deal of sex and violence.

Hugh   A great deal.

Stephen   Lots of sex and violence.

Hugh   That's right. During the sketch, Stephen hits me several times with a golf club.

Stephen   Which of course wouldn't matter except that I hit Hugh very sexily.

Hugh   That's the trouble, you see. He does do it so sexily. I wish you could see it.

Stephen   And then the sketch ends with us going to bed together . . .

Hugh   . . . violently.

Stephen   Extremely violently. Now this raises problems.

Hugh   Not for me.

Stephen   Me neither, but Sir William Rees-Mogg didn't like it a bit, did he?

9

Hugh	Well there was one bit he liked.
Stephen	Yes that's true. He did like it one bit. But he didn't like it a lot of other bits.
Hugh	But I don't want you to think that Sir William's remit with the Broadcasting Standards Council is so sweeping as to be a kind of government thought police.
Stephen	No. The concern is primarily for standards.
Hugh	Standards.
Stephen	For the sake of our children.
Hugh	So, in a generous spirit of give and take, Sir William has taken our sketch.
Stephen	And we've given it to him.
Hugh	And he has written one for us to do instead. Which is free of any gratuitous sex and violence.
Stephen	And shows due and proper regard for decency and standards.
Hugh	Promoting family life and protecting our children.
Stephen	Sir William has called his sketch simply 'Bitchmother, Come Light My Bottom'.
Hugh	And we're going to do it for you now.
Stephen	'Bitchmother, Come Light My Bottom', by Sir William Rees-Mogg.

VOX
POP

Stephen   Oh yes, my wife wears the trousers. No question. But we're hoping to get a second pair some time next year.

Haircut

Stephen is dressed as, and therefore in dramatic terms is, a barber. Hugh enters the shop.

Stephen   Good morning sir.

Hugh   Morning.

Stephen   Yes sir, I do believe we're in for a spell as they used to say in the music halls. Not too hot, but not too mild neither..

Hugh   Mmm.

Stephen   Re the weekend just past, might I enquire as to whether sir was in receipt of an enjoyableness, or did events prove themselves to be of an otherwise nature?

Hugh   Very pleasant thank you.

Stephen   Thank you sir. Very pleasant. Good. Then in presumption of sir's answer, I may take it that sir was for that period without the boundaries of Lincolnshire, wherein, I understand, it rained like a bitch.

Hugh   No, I was nowhere near Lincolnshire.

Stephen   Sir, I am uplifted to hear such news.

Hugh   My wife and I spent the weekend in Hull.

Stephen   Sir is married?

Hugh   Yes.

Stephen   I had literally no idea.

Hugh   Well never mind . . .

Stephen   Will sir at some future time, as yet unspecified,

	forgive me for not having immediately congratulated him on his joyousness in the good tidings department?
Hugh	Of course. I didn't expect you . . .
Stephen	Would sir perhaps consider it to be beyond-boundingly forward of me, on behalf of all the staff here, to send a bouquet of flower-style objects to Mrs Sir?
Hugh	Well that's really not necessary.
Stephen	Sir, since I began as a barber, not thirty-nine years ago, the phrase 'not necessary' has been neither more nor less than as a spur to quicken my actions.
Hugh	Well thank you, that's very kind of you . . .
Stephen	Alright sir. To business. Being one of the shrewdest sirs it has been my privilege to meet, you are no doubt keen to exploit the social and financial advantages inherent in having a hair cut?
Hugh	A haircut, that's right.
Stephen	Of course. A hair cut is a hair enhanced if sir will fail to slash my throatlet for being so old. Now the hair in question is . . . ?
Hugh	What?
Stephen	The hair presently under advisement belongs to . . . ?
Hugh	What do you mean?
Stephen	What do I mean?
Hugh	Yes.
Stephen	Haha. I sneak myself towards the suspicion that sir has cast me as the mouse in his ever popular cat drama.

Hugh	What are you talking about? It's my hair. I want you to cut my hair.
Stephen	Ah. So sir's own hair is the hair upon which this entire transaction is to be founded?
Hugh	Well of course. Why would I come in here to get someone else's hair cut?
Stephen	Sir. Please set fire to my legs if I am trying to make haircutting seem more glamorous than it really is, but may I just say this – you cannot be too careful in my position.
Hugh	Really?
Stephen	Indeed sir. Once and only once, I cut a gentleman's hair against his will. Believe me when I say it was both difficult *and* impossible.
Hugh	No, well it's my hair I want cut.
Stephen	Your hair.
Hugh	Yes.
Stephen	The hair of sir.
Hugh	Yes.
Stephen	Excellent. Then let us proceed to the next and most important of stages. Which one?
Hugh	Which one what?
Stephen	Which of sir's manifold hairs would he care to place in my professional care for the purposes of securing an encutment?
Hugh	Well all of them.
Stephen	All of sir's hairs?
Hugh	Yes.
Stephen	Sir is absolutely sure?
Hugh	Of course I'm sure. What's the matter with you?

Stephen	I seek not to question the drasticity of sir's decision, only to express the profoundness of my humblings at the prospect of such a magnificent task.
Hugh	Well, all of them.
Stephen	All of them. My word.
Hugh	Is that a problem?
Stephen	By no means. I merely hope that sir can find a moment in his otherwise hectic schedule to appreciate that for me to cut every one of sir's hairs represents the snow-capped summit of a barber's career.
Hugh	Well you've done it before, haven't you?
Stephen	Indeed, sir. I once cut all the hairs on a gentleman's head in Cairo, shortly after the War, when the world was in uproar and to a young man everything seemed possible.
Hugh	Once?
Stephen	It would be pointless for me to deny that I was fitter and better-looking then, but let us hope for sir's sake, that the magic has not entirely disappeared up its own rabbit hole. We shall see.
Hugh	Wait a minute. Wait just one cotton-picking minute here.
Stephen	Sir?
Hugh	You've cut someone's hair, all of it that is, once since the war?
Stephen	Would sir have preferred that in the sphere of total hair cuttation, I was to him a virgin?
Hugh	I beg your pardon?
Stephen	That I can respect.

Hugh	What?
Stephen	The desire that we should both of us embark upon this voyage as innocents, wide-eyed travellers in a foreign land, unknowing of our destination, careless of our fate – to emerge somewhere, some day, bruised, tender, a little sad perhaps, but ultimately and joyously alive.
Hugh	Goodbye.
Stephen	Sir is leaving?
Hugh	Yup.
Stephen	Might I be favoured with an explanation as to why?
Hugh	Because I don't believe you have the faintest idea as to how you're going to end this sketch, and I simply don't want to be around when you try. It's going to be painful and embarrassing for both of us, and to be honest I'd much rather it was only painful and embarrassing for you.
Stephen	But sir!
Hugh	What?
Stephen	Sir could not be more mistaken if he tried. I know precisely how this sketch is going to end.
Hugh	Really?
Stephen	Really.
Hugh	Go on then.
Stephen	It might take time.
Hugh	Yes, time and pain and embarrassment. Goodbye.
Stephen	You bastard.
Hugh	Here we go.
Stephen	The number of times I've hung around while you've stumbled on to some pathetic ending.

15

Hugh   You see? You're completely stuck.

Stephen   No I'm not.

Hugh   Ha.

Stephen   Forty-five seconds. I can end this sketch in forty-five seconds.

Hugh   Yeah?

Stephen   Yeah.

Hugh   OK. Forty-five seconds.

Stephen   If sir will resume the seatedness of his posture.

Hugh   Alright.

Stephen   Can I assume that sir is close to the level of maximum comfort?

Hugh   Forty seconds.

Stephen   I will now fetch the necessary tools.

Stephen exits.

Hugh   Haha. It's going to be a chainsaw or some bloody . . . tscch.

Hugh looks at his watch. Stephen does not re-enter.

Long pause. Hugh realises he has been left holding the baby.

Fuck.

Spoonbending with Mr Nude

Hugh and Stephen are sitting in a TV studio. There is a table lamp. Hugh has an annoying accent.

Stephen   Now, Mr Nude, you claim . . .

Hugh   That's right, I do claim, I do . . .

Stephen   Yes, you claim to be able to bend spoons with psychic energy . . .

Hugh   Psychic energy, yes, that is the method I have chosen, to bend spoons, yes.

Stephen   How long have you had this ability?

Hugh   How long, precisely, that's absolutely right.

Stephen   Well?

Hugh   Indeed, you are very sympathetic, thank you. It's very difficult when people are not sympathetic, but you are very sympathetic.

Stephen   Thank you.

Hugh   No, thank *you*.

Stephen   Can you do other things with spoons, apart from bend them?

Hugh   Yes of course I can. I can do anything with a spoon.

Stephen   Can you?

Hugh   Indeed I can. Give me a spoon, and I will give you the world.

Stephen   Well that's an impressive claim, certainly.

Hugh   Thank you.

Stephen	That's alright. Well Mr Nude, we have some spoons here. Perhaps you'd care to give us a demonstration?
Hugh	I am not a circus freak, you know.
Stephen	I realise that.
Hugh	Some people think I am a freak. I am not a freak.
Stephen	Well I'm sure that nobody here . . .
Hugh	'Freak!' They sometimes shout at me in the street.
Stephen	Do they really? That's awful.
Hugh	But you are very sympathetic.
Stephen	Thank you.
Hugh	Thank you.
Stephen	Would you care to have a go at bending this spoon for us?
Hugh	Thank you, yes I will bend this spoon.
Stephen	Ladies and gentlemen, Mr Nude is now going to bend this spoon using psychic energy.
Hugh	That's right, now is when I'm going to bend it.
Stephen	Go ahead, Mr Nude.

Hugh quite plainly bends the spoon with his hands.

Hugh	Thank you very much, you are all very sympathetic.
Stephen	Well the spoon is certainly bent.
Hugh	Of course it is bent. Of course it is. I bent the spoon, so, of course it is bent.
Stephen	Yes, that much is clear and without argument.
Hugh	Forgive me, I am very tired now. To bend a

18

	spoon is very tiring, and I have bent too many spoons today.
Stephen	How many spoons have you bent today?
Hugh	Four spoons today. It is too much. I am not a freak, you know. I am a human being.
Stephen	Forgive me, Mr Nude ...
Hugh	Of course.
Stephen	Thank you.
Hugh	Thank you.
Stephen	But from where I was sitting, it looked rather as if you just bent the spoon with your hands.
Hugh	What are you saying?
Stephen	I'm saying that ...
Hugh	What is this?
Stephen	It's a bent spoon.
Hugh	There.
Stephen	Oh quite, the question is how did you bend it?
Hugh	I don't know how much I like you now.
Stephen	Well, I'm sorry.
Hugh	Before I thought you were very sympathetic ...
Stephen	Well I hope that ...
Hugh	But now, I think you are not so sympathetic. Now, I don't like you.
Stephen	I'm sorry to hear that.
Hugh	At all.
Stephen	Are you sure it isn't 'fraud' that people shout at you in the street, rather than 'freak'?
Hugh	It is you who make the claims. I have always been

Hugh	honest. I bend the spoons with psychic energy, I have told you. I never claimed to be able to bend them with my hands. That is your claim.
Stephen	And you did bend it with your hands.
Hugh	The spoon is bent, that is enough. Perhaps it does flow through my hands this psychic energy of which you claim. It may be. Certainly the spoon is bent. Therefore I bent it.
Stephen	I can bend a spoon with my hands too.
Hugh	I have never said that my powers are unique. Always I have striven to teach the world that anyone may bend a spoon. My book is not expensive.

Stephen bends a spoon.

Stephen	There.
Hugh	To think I found you sympathetic. I hate you now.
Stephen	Well next week I shall be examining the claims of a man who says that in a previous existence he was Education Secretary Kenneth Baker and I shall be talking to a woman who claims she can make flowers grow just by planting seeds in soil and watering them. Until then, wait very quietly in your seats please. Goodnight.
Hugh	*(Simultaneously)* If viewers living in the Matlock and Buxton areas of Derbyshire would be so kind as to inspect their cutlery drawers at home they will find that they contain a bent spoon and an unused Weetabix special offer coupon. I can also reveal that everyone in the town of Datchett over the age of fourteen has a slight itch just above the right thigh which they are scratching as I speak. Thank you.

Critics One

Stephen and Hugh are sitting in swivel chairs, with haircuts. They look and sound nearly as revoltingly smug, smarmy and unpleasant as real critics.

Hugh   Simon Clituris, you watched that sketch ... I assume you were disappointed?

Stephen   Well frankly, I thought it was predictable.

Hugh   You predicted it, did you?

Stephen   Absolutely, and I think that's why it was predictable. Their choice of targets was predictable ...

Hugh   Estate agents ...

Stephen   Where?

Hugh   The target of that last sketch was estate agents.

Stephen   I didn't notice that.

Hugh   And of course their choice of language was predictable ...

Stephen   Precisely. English was a sadly predictable language for them to have chosen.

Hugh   Which is a shame.

Stephen   A great shame. If you don't speak it.

Hugh   A bigger shame if you do.

Stephen   Hahaha.

Hugh   Hahahaha.

Stephen   But I suppose one could have predicted it.

Hugh   I suppose so. Can you predict what their next sketch will be?

Stephen   Oh lord, yes. A parody of 'Treasure Island'. Bound to be.

Cut to something that is as far from being a parody of Treasure Island as is emotionally possible.

VOX
POP

Hugh I can remember exactly what I was doing when I heard the news. I was listening to the news.

Troubleshooters

Stephen and Hugh are being dramatic businessmen.

Hugh   Calm down John, we're not going to get anywhere . . .

Stephen   Don't tell me to calm down. Dammit Peter, I want answers, and I want them fast.

Hugh   Answers? A bit late for all that, don't you think? *(Drinks)*

Stephen   What the hell's happened to you, Peter? You know as well as I do, there's no such word as 'a bit late for all that'.

Hugh   Agreed.

Stephen   So shoot. What've we got?

Hugh   Marjorie wants control of Derwent Enterprises, and from where I'm sitting, she's going to get it.

Stephen   Marjorie? Jesus, Peter, Marjorie's just a kid.

Hugh   Tell that to the board.

Stephen   Watch me. I might just do that. *(Drinks)*

Hugh   Good luck to you.

Stephen   Meaning?

Hugh   They'll laugh in your face, John. Like they did me. Marjorie's got them eating out of her hand.

Stephen   Alright. Then I'll go to old man Derwent himself.

Hugh   Come off it John. No one's even spoken to old man Derwent in years. The man's a recluse. It's hopeless I tell you. Marjorie's won. And she hasn't even fired a shot. *(Drinks)*

23

Stephen   Listen to me, Peter. Marjorie may have won the war, but she hasn't won the battle.

Hugh   Dammit John, you're up to something. I've seen that look before.

Stephen   You're damn right I'm up to something.

Hugh   Dammit.

Stephen   What?

Hugh   What are you up to?

Stephen   Something. I'm up to something.

Hugh   I thought so.

Stephen   I want you on my team for this, Peter.

Hugh   Dammit John, I'm yours, you know that.

Stephen   I haven't finished. It's absolutely mandatory that you buy into my way of working. Things could get a little hairy during the next forty-eight. *(Drinks)*

Hugh   You know me, John. Hairy is as hairy does.

Stephen   Good to hear. Call O'Neill for me, will you? Get him to postpone the meeting.

Hugh   What shall I tell him? *(Drinks)*

Stephen   *(Shouting)* Tell him any damn thing you like – just buy me some time!

Hugh   Dammit John, it's good to have you back.

Stephen   You'd better save the pretty speeches for later, Peter, we've a long night ahead of us. *(Drinks)*

Hugh   Just like old times, eh, John?

Stephen   Sure, Peter, sure.

Hugh   *(Dialling)* You know it's funny. I drove through High Wycombe just the other day . . . *(into phone)* Hello? Peter here. Get me O'Neill.

24

Stephen	And fast.
Hugh	And fast. *(pause)* Say again? Dammit.
Stephen	What?
Hugh	O'Neill's out of town and can't be reached.
Stephen	Dammit to hell and back.
Hugh	Right. Damn blast and double damn.
Stephen	Damn.
Hugh	Want me to try Amsterdam?
Stephen	No.
Hugh	But . . .
Stephen	Come on Peter, you're not thinking straight. Amsterdam's too obvious. Marjorie was never obvious. That's why I loved her.
Hugh	*(Drinks)* By God here's a turn-up. I never thought I'd hear an old warhorse like you talk about love.
Stephen	Love's nothing to be afraid of, Peter. You don't need a Harvard MBA to know that the bedroom and the boardroom are just two sides of the same ballgame. I wonder –
Hugh	Try me. Shoot.
Stephen	Put it together. A block of part-paid ordinaries funnelled through Geneva. A carefully staged release of IDL preference stock through the back door underpinned by a notional rights issue. Who'll be wincing then? *(Drinks)*
Hugh	Dammit John, it's starting to add up. Want me to try Sydney?
Stephen	Come on Peter, stay awake. He'll be in Australia by now.
Hugh	Dammit sideways. Wait a minute. Will they trace it back to us?

25

Stephen	A ploy like that? It'll have Seagrove's handwriting all over it, John.
Hugh	And back again. But that still leaves us with Marjorie.
Stephen	Dammit.
Hugh	*(Whispered mysteriously)* What's she *after*?
Stephen	No point in asking that, Peter. I gave up trying to understand Marjorie a long time ago.
Hugh	Yeah. Women.
Stephen	Marjorie isn't women, Peter.
Hugh	No, of course not, John. Forgive me. I meant no offence.
Stephen	Something I've always wondered. How did you keep Nancy so long?
Hugh	I've never been Nancy, John.
Stephen	No, your wife.
Hugh	Oh Nancy. You know. Rough with the smooth. You work at it. Do your best. Never enough time. Keep on grafting, long hours, you think you know but of course you don't, cover all the angles, they talk about stress, I tell them I'm married to it.
Stephen	Am I right in thinking that you have a daughter?
Hugh	Yup. Henrietta.
Stephen	Did he? Did he really? That must have hurt. Hurt like hell on a jetski.
Hugh	You never had kids of your own, I believe?
Stephen	You're wrong, Peter. You're so wrong.
Hugh	Oh, I beg your pardon.
Stephen	We're sitting in my children at this moment.

Hugh	I may have misheard that, John.
Stephen	The company, Peter.
Hugh	Oh right.
Stephen	I gave everything to this company. *(Suddenly shouting)* Dammit New York should have rung by now!
Hugh	Relax, John. It's still early.
Stephen	I know, Peter. But it's not going to stay early for long.

Stephen goes to the window.

Hugh	New York'll come through, John. I know they will.
Stephen	*(Looking out of the window)* I hope so. There are six million people out there, Peter.
Hugh	Really? What do they want?
Stephen	Who knows? Peter.
Hugh	Yeah.
Stephen	I say we go with it.
Hugh	Agreed.
Stephen	If New York rings, we give them affirmative.
Hugh	I'll tell Susan.
Stephen	Now let's get the hell out of here.
Hugh	Sure?
Stephen	Yeah. I don't think even we two can sustain this level of high intensity work without coming down for a space.
Hugh	Dammit you're right.
Stephen	Besides, I could use a drink.

Gordon and Stuart eat Greek

Stephen (Gordon) and Hugh (Stuart) are sitting at a table in a Greek restaurant. Music plays in the background.

Hugh   Yeah, I like to eat Greek at least once in a time, Gordon. It's a plain cuisine, simply prepared.

Stephen   Yeah, well I'm not averse myself, Stuart.

Hugh   No?

Stephen   Substantially partial to a plate of Greek, as it happens. Substantially partial.

Hugh   Good. *(Indicating menu)* We won't worry about this. I'll chat to the top over-waiter personally. This is just for the walk-in punters.

Stephen   Right you be.

Hugh   Listen to that bazooka music, Gordon. East meets West.

Stephen   Love it.

Hugh   There's a lot to be learned from the Greeks, you know. After all, they gave us the word 'civilization'.

Stephen   I thought that was the Romans.

Hugh   Ethnically the same peoples, Gordon. Also the word 'economics'. Sharp folk, your Greeks. Very sharp.

Stephen   And the word 'genoymeen'.

Hugh   What?

Stephen   They gave us that as well. I suppose we must have just given it back, almost immediately.

28

Hugh	Tough folk, your Hellenics. Hard as the crags and boulders that shape the islands and hills of their landscape.
Stephen	Tssch. Do you know I wouldn't be surprised if there was a lesson in there somewhere?
Hugh	Certainly there is. I've often thought of putting out a paper on the correlation between landscape and business acumen.
Stephen	Great subject, Stu. You could set fire to some arses with a paper like that. The Institute of Executive Salesmen would go ape crazy on all fours for a theory of that sort.
Hugh	I think so, Gordon. I think so. Take my own case. Myself, way back when, my folks hailed from Yorkshire. You see? Limestone uplands, unforgiving moors and scarred dales. An uncompromising, beautiful, hard and wide nurse of men.
Stephen	But you were born in Surrey.
Hugh	The limestone's in my blood. You can see it in the way I do business. Where you from first off, Gordon?
Stephen	Lincolnshire.
Hugh	Huh. You see? Flat, sodden, yielding, chalky, cautious, indecisive, always late for meetings . . .
Stephen	Well Lincolnshire's flat, Stu, yes. But I wouldn't say it was always late for meetings . . .
Hugh	*(Ignoring him)* Yeah, maybe I'll put that paper out after all. Maybe I'll do that.
Stephen	Service is a bit slow.
Hugh	You see, that's the typical lowlander's reaction. That's got Lincolnshire written all over it. You've

got to understand that the Greek does things at his own tempo, Gordon. Natural rhythms and cycles, deep within them. The Yorkshireman in me respects that.

Stephen   Well we don't want to be late for the basketball game, Stuart.

Hugh   *(Shouting)* Service here! Let's get some action at this table!

Waiter arrives. A cheery Greek figure.

Waiter   Good afternoon, my lovely friends.

Hugh   OK, *kalli spera*.

Waiter   Ah. Is lunchtime. You mean *kalli mera*.

Hugh   Well yes, in some dialects, obviously. Now . . .

Waiter   *To piato tees meras chtopothi.*

Hugh   Good, good. So . . .

Stephen   The dish of the day is octopus.

Hugh   I know that, Gordon. Well aware. Where was the octopus caught?

Waiter   Where was it caught? What a question. In the sea.

Hugh   Right. It should be OK then Gordon, if you want to have that.

Waiter   So . . . ?

Stephen   Well *thelo parakalo dolmades kai filetto souvlaki kai nero pagomeno kai ena boukali retsina.*

Waiter   *Entaxi. Kai ya sas, kyrie?*

Hugh   What?

Stephen   What would you like, Stuart?

Hugh   The same. Definitely. The er . . . *parakalo*.

30

Stephen	Δυο
Waiter	Certainly, gentlemen.

Waiter exits.

Hugh	And we'd better order up some wine while we're at it.
Stephen	I did that, Stuart.
Hugh	Oh, of course you did, yeah. I was miles away.
Stephen	He's a bit forward isn't he? All that 'lovely friends' stuff.
Hugh	Well what he's done, Gordon, is recognise a kindred spirit. He's spotted the craggy moorlander in me and he knows that he and I have been nourished by essentially the same granite. Ergo, we're clients to be treated with respect, not your usual walk-in, quick turnover merchants.

Waiter enters, with plates.

Waiter	*Dolmades* for my two beautiful English gentlemen, I think.
Hugh	Great.
Stephen	Looks good.
Waiter	Is very good, my special friends.

Waiter exits.

Stephen	*(Tucking in)* Ha.
Hugh	What is this?
Stephen	Well it's *dolmades*.
Hugh	*Dolmades?*
Stephen	Stuffed vine leaves.

Hugh	Stuffed vine leaves? Is he trying to take us for a ride?
Stephen	It's a classic Greek dish.
Hugh	Classic Greek . . . What am I, a peasant or a busy executive?

Waiter enters.

Waiter	Everything alright, my absolute darlings?
Hugh	Fine thank you.
Stephen	My colleague doesn't like *dolmades*.
Waiter	But you ask for *dolmades*.
Stephen	He didn't know what it was.
Hugh	I knew what . . . hahahaha. Everything's just fine, thank you.

Waiter exits.

Let's get out of here, Gordon. This is just a tourist trap.

Stephen	In Stevenage?
Hugh	Why not?
Stephen	But this is good, Stuart.
Hugh	Wake up, Gordon, wake up! Jesus, they must have seen you coming a mile off.
Stephen	Don't you want your *dolmades?*
Hugh	Do I want to push a stuffed vine leaf through my face? No, incredibly, I don't.
Stephen	Well I'm starving, so if it's all the same with you . . .
Hugh	*(He drinks some wine)* Oh that's it. This wine is corked.

Stephen	It can't be. It's got a metal top.
Hugh	Don't get clever. Just taste it. *(Banging table)* Waiter!
Stephen	Delicious.
Hugh	Delicious? It's got something in it.

Waiter enters.

Waiter	Yes, my excellent friends?
Stephen	*(To Hugh)* It's resinated.
Hugh	Exactly. Waiter, this wine has resinated in the bottle.
Waiter	Yes. Is retsina.
Stephen	It's supposed to be like that, Stu. They add pine needle resin to it . . .
Hugh	Yeah, thanks very much for your input Gordon, but I hope I know my wines. I didn't fork out on an encyclopaedia of world wines for nothing.
Waiter	Retsina. Is very good.
Stephen	It's delicious, Stu.
Hugh	*(Pause)* Well I hope you're going to invite me to the wedding.
Stephen	What?
Waiter	Give me a pardon?
Hugh	You two are getting married, presumably?
Stephen	Stuart . . .
Hugh	No, obviously a six-year friendship goes out the window if you're going to start siding with some Greeko against me.
Waiter	I think maybe everything is not so good for my two lovers.

33

Hugh *(To waiter)* You can cut that out right now.

Stephen Listen Stu . . .

Hugh No you listen, mush. While you were marking time with linguaphone courses of the ancient world, I was pounding the streets of Tiverton learning the selling trade.

Stephen Stu . . .

Hugh While you tanned your hairy arse on the nude beaches of Crete or wherever it was, stuffing vine leaves with a bunch of perverts, I was getting my masters degree in the university of hard knocks and tough surprises. Well mister – I make no apology. To you or your fancy lover boy. *(He makes for the exit)*

Stephen Stu! Where are you going?

Waiter I can bring you an omelette, if you like, sir.

Hugh Forget it. I've had enough, Gordon. I'm going out for an honest British kebab.

VOX
POP

Stephen What I always say to myself is, 'what would Lester Piggott have done in this situation?'

SAS

Stephen is in an SAS uniform, behind the desk of an Army Careers office.

Stephen So you'd like to join the Special Air Service?

Hugh Not really.

Stephen Not really?

Hugh Well, yes alright.

Stephen That's more like it. Height?

Hugh I'm sorry?

Stephen How tall are you?

Hugh Oh. Nine foot six.

Stephen Nine foot six. Good. Weight?

Silence.

Weight?

Silence.

Well?

Hugh I'm waiting.

Stephen Good. You'd be surprised how many applicants are trapped into revealing how heavy they are. And you weigh?

Hugh Three tons.

Stephen Three tons. Sure about that?

Hugh Just over.

Stephen	Alright. Just over three tons. It's as well to be accurate in these matters. Saves complications later on. So. Any particular disabilities?
Hugh	I've got no sense of taste.
Stephen	In what? Films? Music?
Hugh	Food. I can't taste food.
Stephen	Oh dear. That might be a problem.
Hugh	Might that be a problem?
Stephen	I've just said it might. Never mind, let's press on. Any special skills?
Hugh	I look good in black.
Stephen	Excellent. How old are you?
Hugh	Ten and a half.
Stephen	Shoe size?
Hugh	Twenty-eight.
Stephen	Quirks?
Hugh	Muddling up my height and my shoe size. I mean my shoe size and my height. See? I did it again.
Stephen	Well that seems to be OK. How are you at making small talk?
Hugh	Weather and traffic?
Stephen	That sort of thing.
Hugh	I can hold my end up.
Stephen	Correct. Now, are you aware of what the SAS is all about?
Hugh	Not really.
Stephen	I see. Well originally, the SAS was formed as an élite, crack, secret, crack secret assault force, to work behind enemy lines during the war.

Hugh	Right.
Stephen	Of course our role has changed somewhat since then. Nowadays our duties are to act primarily as a masturbatory aid for Lewis Collins and various back-bench MPs.
Hugh	I beg your pardon?
Stephen	I'm afraid so. A worrying number of today's parliamentarians are quite unable to achieve sexual gratification without fantasizing about the SAS. So basically, we have to go round the place being secret and crack and élite, so that these people will be able to keep their marriages intact.
Hugh	Doesn't sound very exciting. Have you got anything else on your cards?
Stephen	Well, the BBC are advertising for someone to go into that room over there.
Hugh	Which one?
Stephen	*(Pointing)* That one, just over there.
Hugh	Alright. I'll give it a go.

Hugh enters room for next sketch.

VOX
POP

Hugh   It's very hard to undo it, though.
So you have to be absolutely sure.

37

Operations

Stephen and Hugh are sitting on stools.

Stephen   So, Hugh, I believe you've found something of interest in one of your magazines.

Hugh   That's right, Stephen. It's a brochure for the Collingwood Hospital.

Stephen   That's a private hospital, isn't it, Hugh?

Hugh   That's right, Stephen. Important point.

Stephen   And it's in London, England, if I remember serves me correctly.

Hugh   That's precisely where it is, Stephen, yes. What excited me, however, as I was looking through this brochure was not where the hospital is, but the services it offers.

Stephen   Medical services, I presume.

Hugh   They do limit themselves by and large to the provision of medical services, Stephen, yes. I dare say they're keen to consolidate in that area before moving out into other leisure activities.

Stephen   That must be sound business practice, in anyone's book?

Hugh   That's right. But anyway, this brochure . . .

Stephen   Ha. I'd almost forgotten.

Hugh   Well that would have been a shame, Stephen, because this brochure contains a full list of the Collingwood Hospital services, and it includes a complete section on the kinds of operations you can have, it you're ever down that way.

38

Stephen	Would you care to read some of them out, Hugh?
Hugh	Of course, Stephen. Just glancing down the page, I find everything from appendectomy to bone marrow replacement, from organ transplants to heart surgery.
Stephen	So, no shortage of choice then, Hugh?
Hugh	That's right. There's something there for everyone. It really is a mouthwatering selection.
Stephen	When are they open?
Hugh	Well this is one of the great things about the Collingwood. They're open twenty-four hours a day.
Stephen	Weekends?
Hugh	Weekends and Bank Holidays.
Stephen	So the Collingwood Hospital might be a good place to take the family?
Hugh	Absolutely, Stephen. There are plenty of operations that are specially tailored for children. For example, having their legs straightened. Mums everywhere I'm sure would love to go for one of their hip replacements, and for Dad . . . well how about some of that heart surgery we mentioned earlier?
Stephen	That sounds like a heck of a weekend. But Hugh?
Hugh	Yes?
Stephen	We haven't mentioned prices.
Hugh	Of course. Prices vary, Stephen, according to the operation you choose . . .
Stephen	I'd imagine they would.
Hugh	Well they do. Basically they start at around four thousand pounds for a tonsilectomy . . .

Stephen	Right.
Hugh	. . . and can go up to as much as sixty thousand for an eight hour operation on the brain.
Stephen	So really, whatever your financial status, there's something at the Collingwood Hospital for you.
Hugh	That's right. There is one proviso I'd add to that.
Stephen	Oh?
Hugh	You should have quite a lot of money.
Stephen	Good point. Whatever your financial status, as long as you've got a lot of money.
Hugh	That's it.
Stephen	And if you haven't? Or if you want to save money?
Hugh	Well, my advice would always be . . . get yourself a stout pair of walking shoes and get out into the beautiful countryside.
Stephen	Thanks, Hugh. Plenty of choices there.

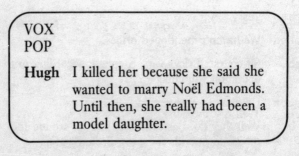

VOX
POP

Hugh I killed her because she said she wanted to marry Noël Edmonds. Until then, she really had been a model daughter.

Sound Name

Stephen is a police sergeant, writing down the particulars of an arrest at the station counter. Hugh is on the other side, looking sheepish.

Stephen   And the vehicle belongs to you, does it sir?

Hugh   Yes.

Stephen   And your name is?

Hugh   Right. Hold on a second. *(Hugh gets a lighter out of his pocket)* Ready?

Stephen   Yes.

Hugh   My name is Derek . . . *(Hugh drops the lighter onto the counter)*

Stephen   What are you doing?

Hugh   That's my name.

Stephen   What is?

Hugh   This. Derek . . . *(Hugh drops the lighter again)*

Stephen   That's your name?

Hugh   Yes.

Stephen   What? Derek *(Stephen drops the lighter)* . . . is your name?

Hugh   Yes.

Stephen   What kind of name is that?

Hugh   Well it's my name.

Stephen   Unusual, isn't it, Mr . . . *(Drops lighter)*?

Hugh	If I had a pound for every time someone's said that . . .
Stephen	And how do you spell . . . *(Drops lighter)*, Mr . . . *(Drops lighter)*?
Hugh	It's as it sounds.
Stephen	Uhuh. Yeah but I wonder if you'd mind actually spelling it for me, would you?
Hugh	Well I mean, can't you just . . .
Stephen	I'd be very grateful. If you wouldn't mind.
Hugh	N–I–P–P–L hyphen E.
Stephen	Nipple.
Hugh	I beg your pardon?
Stephen	Nipple.
Hugh	Nipple? Where? What are you talking about?
Stephen	N–I–P–P–L–E . . .
Hugh	Hyphen E.
Stephen	Hyphen E . . . spells Nipple. In my book. It does not spell . . . *(Drops lighter)*.
Hugh	Have you gone mad? What's the matter with you? I thought the modern policeman was supposed to be a highly trained law enforcement unit. You can't even spell.
Stephen	Alright, Mr Nipple, address?

Hugh looks around.

What's your address?

Hugh	Are you talking to me?
Stephen	Yes.
Hugh	You want to know my address?

Stephen	Please.
Hugh	Or do you want to know Mr Nipple's address, whoever he is?
Stephen	Your address please, sir.
Hugh	Alright. My address is Number twenty-two . . . *(Hugh tapdances, slaps Stephen)* . . . Kings Lynn.
Stephen	Now watch it.
Hugh	What?
Stephen	Just watch it.
Hugh	Watch what, for heaven's sake?
Stephen	You do realise, do you, that assaulting a police officer is an extremely serious offence?
Hugh	Yes, I imagine it probably is. Very serious. But telling a police officer your address, on the other hand, is probably not very serious, is it? Or is it? Perhaps the law's changed since I last looked. Perhaps the Home Secretary has had to take stern measures against the rising tide of people giving their address to policemen whenever they're asked to.
Stephen	Alright. Alright. My fault. Ask a stupid person and you get a stupid answer.
Hugh	I beg your pardon?
Stephen	So, can I just check this with you, Mr . . . *(Drops lighter)* . . . ?
Hugh	What?
Stephen	Just to make sure I've got this right. Your address is . . . number twenty-two . . . *(Tapdances, punches Hugh)* . . . Kings Lynn?
Hugh	No, no, no! What's the matter with you? Are you deaf? It's . . . *(Tapdances, slaps Stephen)* . . . Kings Lynn.

43

Stephen	Oh I'm sorry. I thought you said . . . *(Tapdances, punches Hugh)* . . . Kings Lynn.
Hugh	Well I didn't.
Stephen	My apologies sir. I can't read my own writing.
Hugh	Well get a typewriter.
Stephen	If only we could afford it. Actually, at some angles, this almost looks like . . . twenty-two . . . *(Tapdances, hits Hugh with a cricket bat)* . . . Kings Lynn.
Hugh	That was too hard.
Stephen	Oh I'm sorry sir. You're right. We really should get a typewriter.
Hugh	That was too hard.
Stephen	Well sir, you must admit that it's an unusual address for anyone to get the hang of . . .
Hugh	Never mind the fucking sketch! That was too hard. That really hurt.
Stephen	Oh diddums. Did the nasty actor hit the poor little twerp . . .
Hugh	Fuck off.

Hugh exits.

Stephen *(To camera)* He's just a child really.

VOX
POP

Stephen   Until you've been there, you don't really have any idea what it's like – I shouldn't think. I'm not sure, I've never been there.

44

Spies Two

Stephen is sitting at his desk in the spies' office. Hugh enters carrying a cup of coffee. He puts it down on Stephen's desk.

Stephen Hello, Murchison. Nice to see you.

Hugh Whoops! You gave me rather a fright, Control. Sorry – I nearly upset your coffee there.

Stephen No harm done, I can easily mop up that very small drop and it was very kind of you to bring me some at all. I'm most grateful.

Hugh It was no trouble, I was coming in anyway and I thought 'why not bring in a coffee for Control? It's eleven o'clock, I expect he'd welcome a cup.'

Stephen Greatly appreciated.

Hugh I checked with Valerie and she said you like a little bit of milk, not too much, and no sugar. I hope that's right.

Stephen That's exactly how I like my coffee, Murchison.

Hugh Anyway I ought to tell you why I came in.

Stephen Mm, yes. Was there something you wanted to tell me? Or perhaps you wanted to ask me a question?

Hugh Well a bit of a mixture of both really, Control. Do you remember we decided to put a tail on the new Cultural Attaché at the Russian Embassy?

Stephen Yes, I do remember. I remember the very day we talked about it. We thought he might be a spy working for the KGB, and I said, 'let's follow him around and see if he does anything that might look suspicious'.

Hugh   That's right. We gave him the Codename Big Bad Wolf, and you decided that it would be good to put Philip and his F division in charge of the surveillance.

Stephen   Yes, Operation Coathanger if memory serves me correctly. You were sitting over there – it was quite a rainy day and Philip was standing by the desk, I think.

Hugh   Yes. Though if you remember it was before you moved your desk round this way, so he would have been over there.

Stephen   Oh yes. I must say I do much prefer it like this. I don't think I'll go back. I can see all the door and have quite a nice view over St Giles Circus.

Hugh   Yes. That must be nice. Anyway, it looks as if the Big Bad Wolf probably is a spy after all.

Stephen   Oh dear. Well we certainly feared as much. Just as well we took the trouble to find out. It shows how it's always worth checking things up, isn't it? Has he been meeting known KGB agents then?

Hugh   Yes, he certainly has. As you can see.

Hugh stands there. Stephen puts his hands out and Hugh gives him a blue folder.

Stephen   *(Looking at the folder)* I must say I like this folder. Didn't the old ones used to be blue?

Hugh   Yes. It was Valerie's idea to change to blue. She thought it would brighten the place up a bit.

Stephen   Very nice too. *(Reading)* 'Big Bad Wolf has a Meeting with Colonel Andreyev in John Lewis's.' Did Philip take this photograph himself, do you think?

Hugh   *(Coming round to look)* It certainly looks like Philip's handiwork.

46

Stephen   You can't see which department they're in. I hope Big Bad Wolf isn't stealing any of our secrets or trying to persuade our agents to defect.

Hugh   That would be galling, wouldn't it?

Stephen   I tell you what. You leave this one with me, Murchison.

Hugh   Are you going to tell the Minister?

Stephen   I'll certainly have to do that, yes. Meanwhile Philip had better keep up the surveillance.

Hugh   Would you like me to tell him? I'll be seeing him later today.

Stephen   Would you? That would certainly save me the trouble.

Hugh   No problem at all.

Stephen   Thanks.

Hugh   You're welcome. Anyway, I'd better get back to my office now. The Prague desk has been in a bit of a flap.

Stephen   Uh-oh. Mustn't keep you then.

Hugh   I'll let you know if anything else crops up.

Stephen   That would be appreciated. And thanks again for the coffee. It tasted very nice.

Hugh   Really such a pleasure. See you then, Control.

Stephen   Bye bye, Murchison.

Toaster

Hugh enters an electrical goods shop. Stephen is behind the counter.

Hugh   Hello. I'd like to buy a toaster.

Stephen What sort of toaster are you looking for?

Hugh   I beg your pardon?

Stephen What sort of toaster are you looking for?

Hugh   Oh I see what you mean. Well, ideally I'd like one that's good at toasting bread . . .

Stephen Yes.

Hugh   . . . but can also be used as a weapon.

Stephen A weapon?

Hugh   I beg your pardon?

Stephen A weapon?

Hugh   Oh I see what you mean. Yes, a weapon.

Stephen Mmm. Call me an unrestrained arsewit if you like . . .

Hugh   Perhaps later.

Stephen As you wish. Why would you want to use a toaster as a weapon?

Hugh   I beg your . . .

Stephen Why would you want to use a toaster as a weapon?

Hugh   These are uncertain times. We live in a shifting quicksand of international tension, forever dancing uncertain and fantastical steps on the brink of war.

Stephen Christ.

48

Hugh	I think the optimum choice in the circumstances would be some kind of lightweight throwing toaster.
Stephen	A lightweight throwing toaster?
Hugh	Affirmative. Then I could use it as a weapon.
Stephen	Forgive me if I seem to be labouring the point, but wouldn't it be simpler to use a weapon as a weapon, and use the toaster for toasting?
Hugh	I've already got a weapon.
Stephen	Well doesn't it work?
Hugh	Not as a toaster.
Stephen	Well let me assure you, all our toasters work as toasters.
Hugh	But not as weapons?
Stephen	'Fraid not.
Hugh	Huh. Well that's not going to be much good when they come parachuting into Carshalton.
Stephen	Who?
Hugh	I beg your pardon?
Stephen	Who is going to be parachuting into Carshalton?
Hugh	They are.
Stephen	Who is 'they'?
Hugh	I dunno. I'm not interested in politics.
Stephen	I see.
Hugh	I didn't have this problem with my bed.
Stephen	Mmm. Your bed is a weapon?
Hugh	In the right hands, yes.
Stephen	A lightweight throwing bed?

Hugh	Don't be stupid. It's a seek out and destroy bed. Modified for counter-insurgency operations.
Stephen	Aha.
Hugh	Perfect for the rough terrain surrounding the Carshalton area.
Stephen	I see.
Hugh	The bed shop was most helpful.
Stephen	Well I dare say, but this is a kitchen appliance shop. If you want weaponry, I can't help feeling you'd be better off going to a specialist.
Hugh	What sort of specialist?
Stephen	Don't tempt me to answer that.
Hugh	What do you mean?
Stephen	Nothing. Nothing. I could suggest a garlic-press, I suppose.
Hugh	Semi-automatic, gas-cooled, hand-to-hand, hunter-killer garlic-press?
Stephen	Well, no, it's not much of a weapon really. Unless you're worried about garlics parachuting into Carshalton.
Hugh	I don't at this time have garlics targetted as a priority threat.
Stephen	Had you thought of a down to earth, honest to goodness kitchen knife?
Hugh	A kitchen knife?
Stephen	Yes.

Produces knife.

Hugh	Don't be stupid. You could have someone's eye out with that.

Stephen   I thought that was the idea.

Hugh   Oh no. No no no. You misunderstand me. My whole life is based on the principle that I will never be the aggressor.

Stephen   Really?

Hugh   All I want is to be prepared.

Stephen   To be prepared?

Hugh   To be prepared for when they come parachuting into Carshalton . . .

Stephen   Yes?

Hugh   And also for the moment when I suddenly feel like a piece of toast.

Stephen   I see.

Hugh   You unrestrained arsewit.

Stephen   You're welcome.

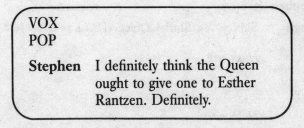

VOX
POP

Stephen   I definitely think the Queen ought to give one to Esther Rantzen. Definitely.

Maternity Ward Ten

Stephen is pacing the corridor of a hospital maternity ward, looking nervous. Hugh puts his head out of a door, wearing a white coat.

Hugh   Mr Conway?

Stephen   No.

Hugh   Ah *(He looks down the corridor)* You are . . . ?

Stephen   Mr Quick.

Hugh   Mr Quick, right, thank you.

Hugh exits.

Pause.

Hugh enters.

Mr Arthur Quick?

Stephen   Noel.

Hugh   I'm sorry?

Stephen   Noel Quick.

Hugh   Noel, yes of course. And your wife is Mrs Mary Quick?

Stephen   Shirley.

Hugh   Shirley, yes. Shirley Quick. Thank you.

Hugh exits.

Pause.

Hugh enters.

Hugh	Mr Quick.
Stephen	Yes?
Hugh	Have you come far?
Stephen	No, well, we're just off the ring road. About twenty minutes.
Hugh	Oh, nice, nice. I say, hasn't your wife got splendid hair?
Stephen	Has she?
Hugh	Oh yes. Fantastic.
Stephen	Well, I suppose it is rather lovely, yes. I hadn't really thought ...
Hugh	Well you should think, Mr Quick. You should. It's lovely hair. Lovely thick, blonde hair.
Stephen	She's got brown hair.
Hugh	Mmm. Lovely.

Hugh exits.

(Shouting off) Brown hair.

Hugh enters.

Lovely thick, brown hair, yes. To be quite frank with you, that's some of the best hair I've seen in a long time.

Stephen	Oh thank you.
Hugh	You're a lucky man, Mr Quick. I'm telling you, that is world-class hair.
Stephen	Is there any chance of seeing her, Doctor?
Hugh	You just can't wait, can you? I don't blame you. With hair like that waiting for you, who wants to hang around in a draughty old corridor?

Stephen	Well quite.
Hugh	Excuse me.

Hugh exits.

Pause.

Hugh enters.

Yes, I always think brown hair looks tremendous on . . . a quite short woman.

Stephen	Well, possibly.
Hugh	Possibly?
Stephen	Of course, my wife's very tall.
Hugh	Ah. You'd say she was very tall would you?
Stephen	Very.

Hugh exits.

Hugh	*(Off)* Very tall. She's very tall, with brown hair.

Hugh enters.

Yes, right. Of course she's tall. Yes. I was thinking of her being quite short, because of course she's lying down at the moment. So she only comes up to my waist. From my point of view, you see, your wife is very short . . . and very wide. But I expect that when you're at home, she stands up quite a lot, and so then you're bound to see more of her tall side.

Stephen	Can I see her?
Hugh	No, you can't.
Stephen	Why not?

54

Hugh   Well, because there's a wall in the way.

Stephen   No. Can I go in and see her?

Hugh   Aha. It's not advisable, frankly. Patients who've just had their tonsils out, are always a bit . . .

Stephen   Tonsils? She's come here to have a baby.

Hugh   Excuse me.

Hugh exits.

(Off) She's come here to have a baby, for Christ's sake!

Hugh enters.

A baby, right. That's a lovely idea. Is it your first?

Stephen   Yes it is, as a matter of fact. We've been trying for quite a long time.

Hugh   I bet you have – with hair like that, phwor, eh? Had any luck so far?

Stephen   What do you mean?

Hugh   With babies. Have you had any luck?

Stephen   Well yes, that's why we're here.

Hugh   Of course, of course.

Stephen   Surely she must have had it by now?

Hugh   Who?

Stephen   My wife. Surely she must have had the baby by now.

Hugh   Oh er . . . hold on.

Hugh exits.

(Off) Well where is it? Well haven't we got *any*? Tscch.

Hugh reenters.

Hugh   Yes she has.

Stephen   She has? That's brilliant! Is it a girl or a boy?

Hugh   It's . . . it's a boy.

Stephen   A boy! Cor! Can I have a look at him?

Hugh   Er . . . here I am, Mr Quick.

Stephen   What do you mean?

Hugh   Er . . . I am your son. I was born about twenty
              minutes ago. Sorry, I should have mentioned
              it earlier.

Stephen   You're my son? What are you talking about?
              Where's the baby?

Hugh   I'm the baby, Mr Quick. Unfortunately I was born
              with a strange disease called Stimtirumtumtum
              which means that I look and sound like an adult
              even though I'm only twenty minutes old. It's very
              rare, but strangely enough it's also quite common.
              Muriel Gray has got it.

Stephen   Muriel Gray?

Hugh   Yes. Only a trained doctor would know that she's
              just six months old.

Stephen   You're mad.

Hugh   Maybe, Mr Quick ... father. But you know, I blame
              the parents.

Stephen   Can I see my wife now?

Hugh   Mother? Of course. We can be a family at last.

Stephen   Shut up.

Hugh   Yes, I always think that fathers should be present
              when their wife's tonsils are being taken out.

56

Prize Poem

*Typical comprehensive school office. Stephen is a
headmaster. He looks worried. There is a knock at the
door. He looks up.*

Stephen   Come.

Enter Hugh.

Ah, Terry, come in, come in.

Hugh   Thank you sir.

Stephen   Well now, do you know why I sent for you?

Hugh   Not really.

Stephen   Not really? Not really? Well, let me see. Firstly,
let me congratulate you on winning the School
Poetry Prize.

Hugh   Thank you sir.

Stephen   Mr Drip tells me that it was the most mature and
exciting poem that he has ever received from a
pupil. Don't suck your thumb boy.

Hugh   I'm not, sir.

Stephen   No, no. It was just a piece of general advice for
the future.

Hugh   Oh I see.

Stephen   Now Terry. Terry, Terry, Terence. I've read your
poem, Terry. I can't pretend to be much of a
judge of poetry, I'm an English teacher, not a
homosexual. But I have to say it worried me.

Hugh   Oh?

57

Stephen   Yes, worried me. I have it here, um: 'Inked Ravens of Despair Claw Holes In The Arse Of The World's Mind', I mean what kind of a title is that?

Hugh   It's my title sir.

Stephen   'Arse Of The World's Mind'? What does that mean? Are you unhappy about something?

Hugh   Well I think that's what the poem explores.

Stephen   Explores? Explores! Oh it explores does it? I see. 'Scrotal threats unhorse a question of flowers', I mean, what's the matter boy? Are you sickening for something? Or is it a girl? Is that the root of it?

Hugh   Well, it's not something I can explain, sir, it's all in the poem.

Stephen   It certainly is all in the poem. 'I asked for answers and got a headful of heroin in return.' Now. Terry. Look at me. Who gave you this heroin? You must tell me: if this is the problem we must do something about it. Don't be afraid to speak out.

Hugh   Well no one.

Stephen   Terry. I'm going to ask you again. It's here. 'I asked for answers and got a headful of heroin.' Now Terry, this is a police matter. Speak out.

Hugh   Sir, no one has given me heroin.

Stephen   So this poem is a lie, is it? A fiction, a fantasy? What's happening?

Hugh   No, it's all true, it's autobiographical.

Stephen   Then, Terry, I must insist. Who has been giving you heroin? Another boy?

Hugh   Well, sir, you have.

Stephen   I have. I have? What are you talking about, you diseased boy? This is rank, standing impertinence. I haven't given anyone heroin. How dare you?

58

Hugh	No, it's a metaphor.
Stephen	Metaphor, how metaphor?
Hugh	It means I came to school to learn, but I just get junk instead of answers.
Stephen	Junk? What do you mean, the JMB syllabus is rigidly adh –
Hugh	It's just an opinion.
Stephen	Oh is it? And is this an opinion too? 'When time fell wanking to the floor, they kicked his teeth'. Time fell wanking to the floor? Is this just put in to shock or is there something personal you wish to discuss with me? Time fell wanking to the floor? What does that mean?
Hugh	It's a quotation.
Stephen	A quotation? What from? It isn't Milton and I'm pretty sure it can't be Wordsworth.
Hugh	It's Bowie.
Stephen	Bowie? Bowie?
Hugh	David Bowie.
Stephen	Oh. And is this David Bowie too: 'My body disgusts, damp grease wafts sweat balls from sweat balls and thigh fungus', I mean do you wash?
Hugh	Of course.
Stephen	Then why does your body disgust you? It seems alright to me. I mean, why can't you write about meadows or something?
Hugh	I've never seen a meadow.
Stephen	Well, what do you think the imagination is for? 'A girl strips in my mind, squeezes my last pumping drop of hope and rolls me over to sleep alone.' You are fifteen, Terry, what is going on inside you?

Hugh	That's what –
Stephen	That's what the poem explores, don't tell me. I can't understand you, I can't understand you.
Hugh	Well you were young once.
Stephen	Yes, in a sense, of course.
Hugh	Didn't you ever feel like that?
Stephen	You mean did I ever want to 'fireball the dead cities of the mind and watch the skin peel and warp'? Then, no, thankfully, I can say I did not. I may have been unhappy from time to time, if I lost my stamp album or broke a penknife, but I didn't write it all down like this and show it to people.
Hugh	Perhaps it might have been better for you if you had.
Stephen	Oh might it, young Terence? I suppose I am one of the 'unhappy bubbles of anal wind popping and winking in the mortal bath' am I?
Hugh	Well –
Stephen	Your silence tells me everything. I am. I'm an unhappy bubble of anal wind.
Hugh	That's just how I see it. That's valid.
Stephen	Valid? Valid? You're not talking about a banknote, you're calling your headmaster an unhappy bubble of anal wind.
Hugh	Well, I'm one too.
Stephen	Oh well, as long as we're all unhappy bubbles of anal wind popping and winking in the mortal bath then of course there's no problem. But I don't propose to advertise the fact to parents. If this is poetry then every lavatory wall in Britain is an anthology. What about *The Oxford Book of Verse*, where's that gone?

60

Hugh	Perhaps that's the lavatory paper.
Stephen	Is that clever?
Hugh	I don't know.
Stephen	I suppose it's another quotation from Derek Bowie is it? I don't understand any more, I don't understand.
Hugh	Never mind, sir. You're a bit frustrated perhaps, it's a lonely job.
Stephen	I am frustrated, yes. It is a lonely job. So lonely. I am assailed by doubts, wracked by fear.
Hugh	Write it down.
Stephen	Eh?
Hugh	Write it down, get it out of your system. 'Assailed by doubts, wracked by fear.'
Stephen	Yes, yes – you think? 'Assailed by doubts and wracked by fear, tossed in a wrecked mucus foam of . . . of . . .'
Hugh	Hatred?
Stephen	Good, good. What about 'steamed loathing'?
Hugh	Better, you're a natural.

Hugh slips away.

Stephen	'. . . wrecked mucus foam of steamed loathing. Snot trails of lust perforate the bowels of my intent. Put on your red shoes, Major Tom, funk to flunky . . . etc . . .

Fade out.

Parent Power

Stephen, a headmaster, is sitting behind a desk. Hugh enters with Michael, a small boy.

Stephen   Ah good morning Michael, good morning Mr Smear.

Hugh   Yes, we'll dispense with the good mornings if you don't mind. I haven't got time for good mornings.

Stephen   As you wish. You wanted to discuss something, I believe?

Hugh   I think you know why I'm here.

Stephen   I don't think I do.

Hugh   *(To Michael)* Tell him.

Michael looks embarrassed.

Stephen   Tell me what?

Hugh   Tell him what you told your mother last night.

Michael   Sexual intercourse can often bring about pregnancy in the adult female.

Stephen   Yes?

Hugh   You heard that, did you?

Stephen   Yes?

Hugh   Well I'd like an explanation, if it's not too much trouble.

Stephen   An explanation of what?

Hugh   An explanation of how my son came to be using language like that in front of his mother.

Stephen	Well I imagine that this is something that Michael learnt in his biology class, isn't that right?
Michael	Yes, sir.
Stephen	Yes I thought so. With Mr Hent. Glad to see some of it's sinking in, Michael.
Michael	Thank you sir.
Hugh	Well I must say this is a turn-up and no mistake.
Stephen	What is?
Hugh	I didn't imagine that you'd be quite so barefaced about it.
Stephen	About what?
Hugh	I came here today to make a complaint about my son being exposed to gutter language in the playground. I am frankly staggered to find that this is something that he's actually been taught in a classroom. I mean what is going on here?
Stephen	We're trying to teach your son . . .
Hugh	Oh are you? Are you indeed?
Stephen	Yes.
Hugh	What? How to embarrass his parents? How to smack himself with heroin?
Stephen	I assure you Mr Smear, we have no intention . . .
Hugh	Call yourself a school?
Stephen	I don't actually call *myself* a school, no.
Hugh	You ought to be ashamed of yourself. Filling a young lad's head with filth like that. Well let me tell you something. About the real world. You're here to provide a service.
Stephen	Quite right.

Hugh   Quite right, yes, well I'm not happy with it. I'm not happy with the service you're providing.

Stephen   Would you rather that Michael didn't attend the biology course?

Hugh   Certainly I would, if those are the kind of lies I can expect to hear repeated at the dinner table.

Stephen   They're not lies, Mr Smear.

Hugh   Oh aren't they? Pregnancy is brought about by sexual intercourse?

Stephen   Yes?

Hugh   Oh Lord save us. So you agree with that?

Stephen   Of course. It's true.

Hugh   True my arse. It's nothing more than a disgusting rumour put about by trendy young people in the sixties.

Stephen   Trendy young people in their sixties?

Hugh   *The* sixties. In *the* sixties. That's when it all started. People like you.

Stephen   Mr Smear, sexual reproduction has been part of the biology syllabus for many years.

Hugh   I don't care about your blasted syllabus. What good is a blasted syllabus out there?

Stephen   Out where?

Hugh   There!

Stephen   The Arkwright Road?

Hugh   Arkwright Jungle, I call it.

Stephen   Well, what would you rather we taught your son, Mr Smear?

Hugh   I would rather . . . I would rather you taught him values, Mr . . .

64

Stephen	Casilingua.
Hugh	Casilingua. Values. Respect. Standards. That's what you're here for. You're not here to poison my son with a lot of randy sextalk.
Stephen	So Michael is definitely your son, is he, Mr Smear?
Hugh	Certainly he's my son.
Stephen	Then it's safe to assume that at some stage you and your wife have had sexual intercourse?
Hugh	*(Pause)* Right. *(Hugh starts to take off his jacket)* That's it. I'm going to knock some sense into you myself.
Stephen	You're going to fight me now, are you?
Hugh	Yes I bloody well am. I'm not going to stand for this.
Stephen	Do you mind if I do? *(Rises to his feet)*
Hugh	Talking like that in front of the boy. You're a bloody disgrace.
Stephen	Mr Smear, let me ask you this. How could Michael be your son, if you haven't had sexual intercourse?
Hugh	Michael . . .
Stephen	Yes?
Hugh	Michael is my son in the normal way.
Stephen	In the normal way?
Hugh	Yes.
Stephen	And what is the normal way to have a son, in your opinion?
Hugh	If you're trying to trick me into sexy talk . . .
Stephen	I'm not.

Hugh	The normal way to have a son is ... to get married.
Stephen	Yes?
Hugh	Buy a house and get properly settled in.
Stephen	Yes.
Hugh	Furniture and so on, and then ... wait for a bit.
Stephen	Ah.
Hugh	Make sure you eat properly. Three hot meals a day.
Stephen	So Michael just sort of turned up, did he?
Hugh	Er ... well of course it's a few years ago now, but yes I think one day he was just there.
Stephen	And you and your wife have never enjoyed sexual intimacy of any kind?
Hugh	Yes, it's very hard for you to believe isn't it, that there are still some people left who can bring a son into this world without recourse to cannabis and government handouts?
Stephen	Well I really don't know what to say.
Hugh	I bet you don't: It's not every day a consumer stands up to you and makes demands is it?
Stephen	Not of this nature no.
Hugh	Yes, well. Welcome to the harsh realities of the market-place, Mr Casilingua.
Stephen	OK. Well, what would you like me to do?
Hugh	It's obvious isn't it? If I go into Littlewoods and tell them I'm not satisfied with a cardigan, say, they'll change it for me. And gladly.
Stephen	You want another son?
Hugh	Certainly I do. Mine is soiled now.

66

Stephen   Well I'm afraid we haven't got any spare sons here, just at the moment.

Hugh   Well what have you got of equal value?

Stephen   Um – there are some locusts in the biology lab.

Hugh   Locusts, hmm. Do I have your assurance that one of these locusts will not embarrass Mrs Smear at table with foul language?

Stephen   I think I can go that far.

Hugh   Well that's something. How many of them are there?

Stephen   Two . . . at the moment.

Hugh   What d'you mean 'at the moment'?

Stephen   Well, it's just that these locusts are married, they've bought the cage, and some furniture, and they're having three meals a day.

Hugh   Hot meals?

Stephen   Warmish.

Hugh   So Mrs Smear might be a grandmother one day?

Stephen   Very possibly.

Hugh   *(Pleased)* She'd like that.

VOX
POP

Stephen   A good smack in the face. She deserves it.

Chatshow

Hugh is a young and surprisingly handsome chat-show host on a young and surprisingly awful Channel Four chat-show. He is behind his desk.

Hugh   *(In reference to whatever sketch has finished)* Well that was the unmistakable sound. Right, my next guest wrote his first novel back in 1972, the year of loons and flares and Suzie Quatro and the Glitter Band and all that stuff. He's been writing ever since, got a new one coming out now. Bit of a cult dude with the Saporo and sushimi set, so let's say a big 'hi!' to Richard Morley!

Enter slightly nervous and serious looking Stephen to absurdly brash music. Hugh does ludicrous jive handshake.

Right, Richard, welcome, sit down, take the weight off your paragraphs.

Stephen looks bewildered by this peculiar joke.

So tell me, this novel, what's it called?

Stephen   The novel I've just written is called *The Emperor of Disgust.*

Hugh   *The Emperor of Disgust.* Sounds pretty heavy.

Stephen   Heavy?

Hugh   What's it about?

Stephen   You haven't read it?

Hugh   Well, for the viewers, you know. They haven't,

obviously. It isn't published till tomorrow is it?
How can they have done!!!

Hugh punches Stephen on the arm.

Stephen   Oh, I see. Well it isn't very easy to tell you the
plot precisely because it is rather complicated.

Hugh   Highbrow stuff I'll bet. Where's it set?

Stephen   Set? Well the action of the novel takes place over
several centuries and a number of different –

Hugh   Tell me, do you use a word processor? Thing I've
always wanted to know about writers, you know,
how they set about it. Pencil, pen, typewriter.
All that.

Stephen   Well I use a word processor as a matter of fact. I
used to use a typewriter, but –

Hugh   How many novels then, have you had, in fact,
published?

Stephen   *The Emperor of Disgust* will be my seventh.

Hugh   Seventh? You take it pretty seriously, then?

Stephen   Yes, yes indeed I do. I do take it seriously. Very
seriously. It's my job you see. My living.

Hugh   Right. Right. Yeah. Tell me, where do you get
your characters from? From real life?

Stephen   Well usually I suppose they're an amalgam,
you know.

Hugh   You gonna put me in one of your books then?

Stephen   Well I think I might actually.

Hugh   *(Thrilled with the idea)* Yeah!?

Stephen   Yes. I really think you are one of the most
repellent and flatulent-minded people I've ever
met. In many respects ideal fodder for the novelist.

69

Hugh laughs in an 'isn't this geezer just brilliant?'
kind of a way.

Stephen   I don't know what you're laughing at, I find you
mindless, vapid and irrelevant.

Hugh   *(Still laughing)* Seriously, Richard, what's the –

Stephen   I am being serious, you repulsive ball of spittle.
And who the hell told you you could call me
Richard? You're rotting in hell and you haven't the
faintest idea of it, have you?

Hugh   The last book you wrote . . .

Stephen   Last book I wrote! You haven't a clue about the
last book I wrote have you, except from what that
daffy researcher you sent round tells you? Your
head is crammed with so much pappy drivel and
greasy bigotry and brash ignorance that there isn't
room in it for one single idea, is there?

Hugh   This is brilliant.

Stephen   Oh it's brilliant is it? It's 'good television' I
suppose. It shows you at the cutting edge of
dangerous broadcasting. You're about as dangerous
as a chocolate 'Hob Nob'.

Hugh mugs to the camera.

Look at you, sitting there like a . . . like a fat,
smug . . . a fat smug . . . *(Breaking out of character
and talking to someone off camera)* Sorry I've
forgotten the next bit, 'a fat smug . . .'

Hugh   *(Also addressing someone off)* Vince, we go live on air
in ten minutes, I thought he knew his lines. What's
going on?

Stephen   Sorry, I'm a bit nervous.

Hugh   *(Coaching)* 'A fat smug git who's just won a . . .'

Stephen   *(With Hugh coaching)* Oh yes, a fat smug git who's just won a BAFTA. Have you any idea how degrading and demeaning to the human spirit people like you are?

Hugh   Great, then I'll ask you where your book is on sale, how much it costs and we'll play you out.

Stephen   Alright.

Hugh   Then I'll do a bit of chat, 'blah-di-blah-di-blah-di-blah' and bang, bang bang. And, what's next?

VOX
POP

Hugh   Sex and violence, really. That kind of thing. We're a small company, but things are very busy at the moment.

Doctor Tobacco

Doctor's surgery – yes I know, but I'm afraid that's where we are.

Hugh is having his chest listened to.

Stephen   Say 'ninety-nine'.

Hugh   Ninety-nine.

Stephen   Good. Say 'thank you'.

Hugh   Thank you.

Stephen   Say 'breasts'.

Hugh   Breasts.

Stephen   Mmm. 'R'.

Hugh   'R'.

Stephen   Good.

Hugh   Good.

Stephen   Well, if you'd like to do your shirt up now Mr Pepperdyne.

Hugh   Everything as it should be?

Stephen   Nothing too serious, you'll be glad to hear. You say that you've been having a little trouble breathing at night?

Hugh   That's right.

Stephen   Been bringing up any sputum?

Hugh   Er, not really.

Stephen   Any yellow or green phlegm . . . blood?

Hugh	No.
Stephen	Tightening of the chest?
Hugh	Well a little I suppose.
Stephen	Headaches?
Hugh	Apart from the children, you mean? Not really.

They both laugh weakly.

Stephen	Right. I want to try you on a course of these: one twenty times a day. Have you ever taken them before?

Gets out a plain cigarette from a drawer.

Hugh	Um – what is it?
Stephen	It's a simple nicotinal arsenous monoxid preparation taken bronchially as an infumation.
Hugh	Infumation?
Stephen	Yes, you just light the end and breathe in.
Hugh	What, like cigarettes?
Stephen	You know them, then? Yes, actually, it's a bit hard to admit, but they're basically a herbal remedy.
Hugh	Oh, herbal cigarettes.
Stephen	That's right. A leaf originally from the Americas I believe, called tobacco.
Hugh	But medicated.
Stephen	Medicated? No.
Hugh	These are ordinary cigarettes?
Stephen	That's right.
Hugh	But they're terribly bad for you aren't they?

73

Stephen   I hardly think I would be prescribing them if they were bad for you.

Hugh   Twenty a day?

Stephen   Yes, ideally moving on to about thirty or forty.

Hugh   But they give you lung cancer and bronchitis and emphysema.

Stephen   Where on earth did you get that idea?

Hugh   Everyone knows that.

Stephen   Are you a doctor?

Hugh   No, but it stands to reason doesn't it?

Stephen   What on earth are you talking about? 'Stands to reason.' You wouldn't even know what a pair of lungs *did* if a doctor hadn't told you. It's taken mankind thousands of years to work out what the heart is for, what a blood vessel is, what the kidneys do, and now you're telling me because you've read a few weedy magazine articles that you know more about the human body than a doctor?

Hugh   Well no, but – it can't be natural, can it?

Stephen   Perfectly natural leaf.

Hugh   Yes but setting light to it and inhaling the smoke, I mean . . .

Stephen   More natural than Baked Alaska or nylon socks.

Hugh   Yes but you don't inhale nylon socks. At least I don't.

Stephen   You wear them next to the skin.

Hugh   But you can't seriously be recommending cigarettes.

Stephen   Why the buggery sod not? A bit of leaf smoke to loosen the lungs, ease that tightness and clear the head. Perfectly sound.

74

Hugh	I suppose you're going to tell me that cholesterol isn't bad for you next.
Stephen	What's cholesterol?
Hugh	It's ... well, you know –
Stephen	Yes I know perfectly well what it is, but I don't suppose you'd so much as heard of it until a few years ago. You'd die without the stuff.
Hugh	Yes but too much is bad for you.
Stephen	Well of course too much is bad for you, that's what 'too much' means you blithering twat. If you had too much water it would be bad for you, wouldn't it? 'Too much' precisely means that quantity which is excessive, that's what it means. Could you ever say 'too much water is good for you'? I mean if it's too much it's too much. Too much of anything is too much. Obviously. Jesus.
Hugh	But I thought the balance of informed medical opinion held that –
Stephen	You thought, you thought. You didn't think, did you? Cigarettes are healing, natural and effective.
Hugh	If you don't mind I think I'd like a second opinion.
Stephen	That's your privilege.
Hugh	Right.
Stephen	*(Pause)* My second opinion is that they are also cheap, nutritious and stylish.
Hugh	Really?
Stephen	And if you're interested in a third opinion they're soothing, harmless and sexy.
Hugh	Well, I must say that does seem to clinch it.
Stephen	Alright then. So twenty a day, rising over the week.

Hugh	And the tightness in the chest?
Stephen	Should disappear completely.
Hugh	Tremendous. Well you're the doctor.
Stephen	What?
Hugh	You're the doctor.
Stephen	Whatever gave you that idea?
Hugh	Well I mean – you did.
Stephen	God, you are pathetic aren't you?
Hugh	Um.
Stephen	I'm a tobacconist. Isn't it obvious?
Hugh	But the –
Stephen	Yes, it looks more like a doctor's surgery than a tobacconist's.
Hugh	Why?
Stephen	Why? Because you're the kind of idiot that falls for that sort of thing. It's the same reason that cosmetics sales staff wear white coats, because pratts like you think a Swiss name and something called a 'skin treatment' must be better for you than a tub of cold cream which is all you're in fact getting. You're a credulous git, Mr Pepperdyne. A stethoscope and a plausible manner doesn't make me a doctor. I'm a conman and you're a moron.
Hugh	You are a doctor then?
Stephen	Could be. What do you think?
Hugh	You really want to know?
Stephen	I'd be fascinated.
Hugh	I think you've taken a reasonably good idea and overworked it. I think what started out as a fairly interesting and amusing statement about our

susceptibility to received ideas has become
something vague, ill-thought out and rambling.
And I think it's time to finish it.

Stephen   Well do you? I think you've comp –

Blackout

Remembering Lines

Hugh and Stephen are on set.

Hugh We'd like to do a sketch for you now entitled, quite simply, 'Jack Nimnock Goes Shopping In the Heart of Norwich'.

Stephen That's right.

They each go to one side of the set and start to walk towards each other. As they pass they recognise one another.

Jack! Jack Nimnock! How are you?

Hugh Neville! I'm fine, fine. How are you?

Stephen Oh mustn't grumble. So what are you up to now?

Hugh Oh this and that.

Stephen Right. Right. So tell me, how's Mary?

Hugh looks blank. Stephen speaks sotto voce.

Mary and I are divorced.

Hugh Mary and I are divorced.

Stephen Divorced? I'm sorry to hear that, Jack. When did this happen?

Hugh again looks blank.

When did this happen?

Hugh A couple of days ago.

Stephen *(Sotto voce)* Years.

Hugh Pardon?

Stephen	*(Sotto voce)* You were divorced a couple of *years* ago.
Hugh	A couple of years ago. Not days, Neville, as I initially suggested, but years.
Stephen	Well this is terrible news, Jack, terrible. Whose idea was it, if you don't mind me asking?

Hugh looks blank again.

Hugh	What?
Stephen	The divorce. Was it your idea or Mary's? *(Sotto voce)* Mine.
Hugh	Mine.
Stephen	Yours?
Hugh	Yours?
Stephen	Mine.
Hugh	Mine.
Stephen	So it was your idea?
Hugh	So it was *your* idea?
Stephen	I see. How did Mary take it?

Hugh looks blank yet again. Stephen starts to look annoyed.

	(Semi sotto voce) Not too badly at first.
Hugh	Not too badly at first.
Stephen	*(Semi sotto voce)* But I think she's pretty low at the moment.
Hugh	But at the moment I think she's pretty low.
Stephen	And how about you?
Hugh	Erm . . . don't tell me.
Stephen	You had a nervous breakdown.

Hugh   Oh yes, I had a nervous breakdown and went into shock and when I recovered I found I'd completely lost my voice.

Stephen   Memory!

Hugh   Memory, I'd completely lost my memory –

Pause.

Stephen   *(Under)* And now I can't remember a thing . . .

Hugh   *(Under)* I know, I know, that was a pause. *(Out loud)* And now I can't remember a thing about that period of my life.

Stephen   That's terrible, so had Mary been cheating on you then?

Hugh   Well . . .

Stephen   *(Whispering)* I've forgotten.

Hugh   *(Whispering)* So have I.

Stephen   No, *you've forgotten.*

Hugh   Oh I see. I've forgotten. She might have been but I just can't . . . um . . . persuade?

Stephen   *(Hissing)* No, remember!

Hugh   November. I'm a . . .

Stephen   *(Walking off)* Git.

Hugh   I'm a git. I'm a git, that's right –

Embarrassed at Stephen's disappearance.

              – right, well cheerio then Neville. It was good seeing you after all these . . . . . . er . . .

Stephen   *(Off yelling loudly)* Years!!!

Hugh   Years! That's right.

Beggar

Hugh is a beggar. Tatty beard, old raincoat – pretty
sordid. He has a small cloth cap on the ground and
is playing the mouth organ. Stephen, dressed like a
plutocrat, passes near him. He stops in amazement
and stares at Hugh. Hugh starts to get rather
discomfited by this.

Stephen   What on earth are you doing? What on earth are
you doing?

Hugh   What do you mean?

Stephen   What is that cloth cap there for?

Hugh   Well it's for the money.

Stephen   Money? What money? I mean, what are you *doing*?

Hugh   I'm busking, aren't I?

Stephen   Busking? Busking? You're busking? What do you
mean you're busking?

Hugh   I play the mouth organ and people give me money.

Stephen   Money? They give you money? For playing the
mouth organ? People give you money for playing
like that? They actually give you money? They
pay you?

Hugh   Some people do. No harm in that.

Stephen   No harm in that? No harm in that he says. People
are prepared to give you money for standing on
a pavement and blowing through spittle? It's
unbelievable.

Hugh   Look if you don't like it, you don't have to listen
or give me anything.

Stephen   Don't like it? How could I like it? It's revolting.
It's the most disgusting and pathetic noise I've
ever heard. And people give you money for it?

Hugh   Well it's kindness as well, isn't it? They're just
being kind.

Stephen   Just being kind? But surely if they were just
being kind they'd put a bullet through your head,
wouldn't they? That's what I'd call being kind. Put
you out of your misery.

Hugh   I'm not that miserable. I quite enjoy it. People are
nice to me.

Stephen   Not miserable? Not miserable? How can you be
not miserable, look at you, your clothes are in rags,
you smell disgusting, how can you be anything
other than miserable?

Hugh   You're very insulting, you know.

Stephen   Yes of course I know. Do you think I wasn't aware
of the fact? Of course I'm insulting. I'm very
insulting indeed, especially to smelly, squalid poor
people who play the harmonica badly.

Hugh   We share the same planet, why can't you
let me be?

Stephen   Share the same planet? What are you saying,
'share the same planet'? The planet I inhabit is
full of restaurants, fast cars, high level finance,
holidays in Barbados and fine wine. Your planet
is full of bottles of meths, howling harmonicas,
smelliness and grimy doss-houses. It's not the
same planet at all. How dare you suggest that it's
the same planet?

Hugh   You may not think they're the same planet but they
are. You couldn't have one without the other.

Stephen   What are you talking about couldn't have one

82

	without the other? What are you talking about? Are you saying I depend upon you?
Hugh	Course you do. All your wealth is entirely propped up on the rotting hulk of my poverty – and one day it will give way and you'll come crashing down with it.
Stephen	Rotting hulk? Have you gone mad? Is this communist talk? Are you a communist? Do you want me to call a policeman?
Hugh	It's not a crime to be a communist. Anyway I'm not.
Stephen	Not a crime? Not a crime? Have you gone howling mad, not a crime. This is 1988, of course it's a crime. Communists are the enemies of democracy, they are criminals.
Hugh	Well what's so good about democracy?
Stephen	What's so good about democracy? What's so good about democracy he asks? It's freedom of speech and thought and belief, that's what's so good about it, you degraded heap of smelliness. Now get out of my way before I set fire to you. Get a job, clean yourself up. It's demeaning to have a pile of litter playing the harmonica at one.

Stephen turns and moves off.

Hugh	*(Behind him, removing beard)* Wait!
Stephen	Wait? Wait for what?
Hugh	*(Pointing straight into the camera)* You see that?
Stephen	What? See what? What have you done with your beard, what is the matter with you? Have you gone mad? See what?
Hugh	*(Laughing)* You don't recognise me, do you?

83

Stephen   Recognise you? No I don't recognise you. Of course I don't recognise you, why should I?

Hugh   Do you ever watch a television programme called 'On The Streets With Bibby'?

Stephen   'On The Streets With Bibby'? Oh, the one with the hidden camera, you mean?
(Suddenly terrified) My God, you're not Robert Bibby are you?

Hugh   *(Sinking down back onto the street)* No, but I might have been.

Little Chat

Hugh   Father?

Stephen   Yes?

Hugh   I've been thinking.

Stephen   Oh yes.

Hugh   You know how you said that Mother had gone to live with Jesus?

Stephen   Yes.

Hugh   Well I don't think that can be right.

Stephen   Oh?

Hugh   Yes. Because I saw Mother last night.

Stephen   You what?

Hugh   Yes. In Asda. And the man she was with was nothing like Jesus at all.

Stephen   *(Putting down newspaper)* Look, Jeremy, I think it may well be time that you and I had a little talk.

Hugh   Aren't we having one now, then?

Stephen   Well, yes, as a matter of fact we are. That's quite right. Good. How old are you now Jeremy?

Hugh   Thirty-one.

Stephen   Thirty-one, eh? When I first told you that Mummy had gone to live with Jesus, how old were you then, eh?

Hugh   Twenty-seven.

Stephen   Yes, well, goodness me, there we are you see. Twenty-seven. Time flies doesn't it? My goodness word me yes. There you are. Well now. When I told you what I told you it was a little bit of a fib.

Hugh	Oh.
Stephen	Yes.
Hugh	You told me a fib.
Stephen	Well it was to spare you hurt, son. You see Mummy didn't go to live with Jesus at all.
Hugh	As I rightly guessed.
Stephen	As you rightly guessed. What really happened was that Mummy died.
Hugh	Died?
Stephen	Yes. She died.
Hugh	But I saw her in Asda.
Stephen	No, you saw someone who looked a little bit like her.
Hugh	Oh.
Stephen	You had to know sooner or later.
Hugh	How did . . . how did Mummy die then?
Stephen	It's a sad story but you should know.
Hugh	Yes?
Stephen	I killed her.
Hugh	You killed her?
Stephen	Yes.
Hugh	Why?
Stephen	Why? Because she was screwing everything in trousers.
Hugh	Oh.
Stephen	*(Returning to paper)* You see?
Hugh	Yes, Daddy.

86

1. Graham Gooch's aggressive appeal fails to impress umpire Jack Shepherd. Tendulkar went on to make an unbeaten 143.

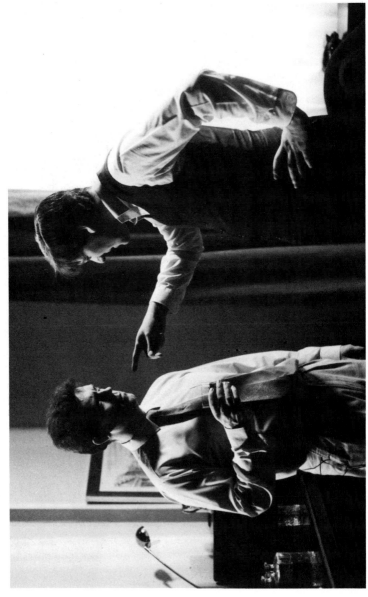

2. London Transport Chief Sir Jack Perrelman explains underground zoning to a group of sixth formers from St Alan's.

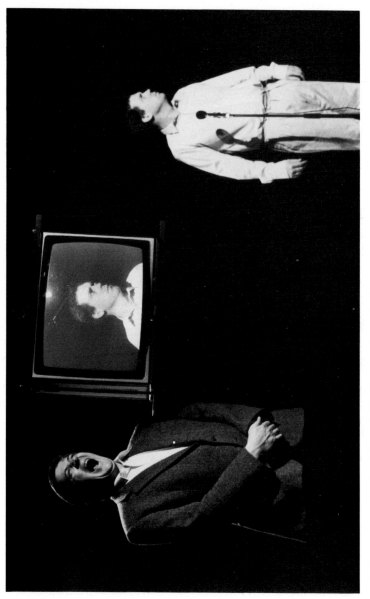

3. As the museum attendant's body jackknifed in a rictus of pain, Sherman made for the control room at a dead run.

4. This shows the gender difference even more clearly.
Note the distended folds (or flaps).

5. Papal greed? A seventeen-mile tailback at junction 14.

6. The USS Tomahawk prepares to embark on Operation 'Butt Kick'.

5. Papal greed? A seventeen-mile tailback at junction 14.

6. The USS Tomahawk prepares to embark on Operation 'Butt Kick'.

7. This was taken with a Nikon F4 at 5.6, with an exposure of 1/500. A diffusion filter was used and the subject's nipples lightly brushed with baby oil. Note the matted dried-on effect.

8. The main restaurant offers relaxed dining
in a traditional atmosphere. The Butty Bar
is Doncaster's premier rendezvous.
A great place to meet people and enjoy a
light informal screw.

Lavatories

Stephen   Lavatories. Love them or loathe them. They're here to stay. We use them, we lavish our affection on them: we clean them, polish them, some of us spend up to half our lives in them. We read specialist lavatory magazines, spend money on the latest models with air-conditioning, stereos and two-speed wipers. Some of us even race them –

Hugh   *(Whispering)* Cars.

Stephen   What?

Hugh   You mean cars, not lavatories.

Stephen   *(Studying script)* Oh yes. Cars. How much do we know about them? We sit in them once a day and trust them to carry our effluent away, safely, cleanly, efficiently. Whether they're porcelain, plastic or fibre-glass, lever or button flush we expect them to –

Hugh   Lavatories. You mean lavatories.

Stephen   Oh yes.

Hugh   T!

Stephen   The beginnings of the modern lavatory were humble enough. In 1793 Johannes Krell of Leipzig constructed the first simple metal cabinet, using inert gases condensing to cool the cabinet to three degrees centigrade. The first dew-bin, or salad crisper started to appear in lavatories –

Hugh   Fridges. You're talking about fridges.

Stephen   Oh yes. Fridges. Like them or loathe them, you can't ignore them. Everyone's talking about them. Whether you're buying or selling a property, sooner or later you'll come in contact with a

fridge. Their commission is an important part of your house budget –

Hugh   Estate agents. You're talking about estate agents.

Stephen   Estate agents. You can't live with them, you can't live with them. The first sign of these nasty, purulent sores appeared round about 1894. With their jangling keys, nasty suits, revolting beards, moustaches and tinted spectacles, estate agents roam the land causing perturbation and despair. If you try and kill them, you're put in prison: if you try and talk to them, you vomit. There's only one thing worse than an estate agent but at least that can be safely lanced, drained and surgically dressed. Estate agents. Love them or loathe them, you'd be mad not to loathe them.

Hugh   That's better.

VOX
POP

Hugh   I just loved the Beetles. They had hundreds of different kinds. Blue ones, black ones, yellow ones, two-tone, cabriolet. They had one with fuel injection.

Information

Stephen is sitting behind a desk with an 'information' sign on it. Hugh enters.

Hugh   Good morning.

Stephen   Good morning.

Hugh   Good morning.

Stephen   Right. Can I help you?

Hugh   Yes. Your face my arse.

Stephen   No, I said can I help you?

Hugh   Oh. I'd like some information, please.

Stephen   Yes.

Hugh   Well?

Stephen   Well what?

Hugh   I'd like some information, please.

Stephen   Yes. What information would you like?

Hugh   Well I don't know. What have you got?

Stephen   I beg your pardon?

Hugh   What information have you got?

Stephen   Well, all sorts.

Hugh   Such as?

Stephen   Such as ... the average weight of a rabbit.

Hugh   Well I never knew that.

Stephen   What?

Hugh   I never knew rabbits had an average weight.

Stephen	Oh yes.
Hugh	Have you got any other information?
Stephen	Of course. But you've got to ask me questions, you see.
Hugh	And you'll tell me the answers . . . ?
Stephen	That's right.
Hugh	. . . if I ask the questions. Right. What's the name . . . ?
Stephen	Yes?
Hugh	What's the name of the man who taught me Geography at school?
Stephen	I'm afraid that's hardly the kind of thing . . .
Hugh	Aha.
Stephen	Tscch. Alright. His name was Colin Drip.
Hugh	That's right.
Stephen	Drippy, you used to call him.
Hugh	Drippy. Cor, that takes me back a bit. Now, there was a bloke in our class – tsch, what was his name . . .
Stephen	Adams, Attersham, Bennet, Connor, Fredericks, Hodson . . .
Hugh	Hodson! That's it, that's it. Ned Hodson. Blimey, he used to drive old Drippy up the wall. D'you know what he used to do?
Stephen	Yes.
Hugh	Oh. Cor. I wonder what happened to him?
Stephen	He married a girl called Susan Trite, and they now live in Fenton, near Worcester.
Hugh	I don't think I ever met her.
Stephen	Yes you did. July the fourth, 1972, you sat next

to her on a twenty-nine bus down Garboldisham Road and she told you about the Bay City Rollers. You were in love with her until the following Wednesday.

Hugh Hm. You've got quite a lot of information, then?

Stephen We try to provide a service. Anything else?

Hugh Yes please. Can you tell me . . .

Stephen Yes?

Hugh Can you tell me how to be happy?

Stephen How to be happy?

Hugh How to be happy.

Stephen I'm afraid to say that information may be restricted.

Hugh Oh. You do have it, though?

Stephen Oh yes.

Hugh But it's restricted?

Stephen I'm afraid so. Sorry.

Hugh Contented?

Stephen Yes thank you.

Hugh No, any information on how to be contented?

Stephen Oh I see. Yes, we've got information on that.

Hugh Can I have it?

Stephen I'm afraid it's a secret.

Hugh Oh, go on.

Stephen Alright. The secret of contentment is . . .

Hugh Yes?

Stephen Don't ask questions.

Open University

Stephen addresses the camera.

Stephen You know, some of the funniest things that happen in television never actually make it to the screen. They're the out-takes, or bloopers, that we all get so embarrassed about. Here's one of my all-time favourites, from an edition of the Open University, recorded in 1979.

Cut to:

Possibly black and white scene of Hugh standing in front of a blackboard with a lot of incomprehensible symbols on it. He is looking appallingly early seventies, paisley, loons etc.

Hugh So that if we increase the non-reflexive integers in the equation by a marginal quantity denoted by D5, we can see that the parallel quantities D7 and D3 are inverted in the same direction, which gives us a resultant modular quantity of minus 0.567359. Now this should begin to give us a clue as to where the next . . .

Stephen enters, dressed as a floor manager, also in a paisley shirt and wide flares. He is laughing.

Stephen Sorry Brian.

Hugh That's alright. What's happened?

Stephen You said '0.567359'.

Hugh I didn't, did I?

Stephen   Yes. *(Laughing violently)* It should have been '0.567395'.

Hugh   Oh no. Oh I don't believe it.

They both laugh hysterically. We hear a succession of bleeps as they swear good-naturedly about the stupidity of the mistake.

Cut to:

Stephen   *(Wiping his eyes)* Marvellous, absolutely marvellous.

VOX
POP

Hugh   My wife and I were thinking of going to Ireland personally, to see what all the fuss is about. But we couldn't face having all the injections.

Spies Three

Stephen is behind his desk in the spies office when Hugh enters.

Hugh   Morning Control.

Stephen Oh. Hello Tony. Come in.

Hugh   Thank you, I will come in, just for the now.

Stephen I expect you've heard the news?

Hugh   Well everything is in quite an uproar. You know what rumours are.

Stephen Yes, it's terrible isn't it, how they spread? I don't know. I sometimes think that if I believed every rumour I heard I'd be believing some things that aren't true at all.

Hugh   T.

Slight pause.

Stephen Anyway, you'll have to forgive me if I yawn a bit during today, what with one thing and another I didn't get too much sleep last night.

Hugh   Poor you, you must be exhausted, or very tired at least, or is that wrong?

Stephen No. I am tired, that's quite right.

Hugh   So perhaps you might tell me exactly what happened, Control, unless you're too tired.

Stephen No, I'd be happy to fill you in, that way you won't have to rely on departmental rumours, will you?

Hugh   No. And that would be a great convenience.

94

Stephen	Well, we picked up Costain last night.
Hugh	I'd gathered as much from the rumours, but I wasn't sure whether it was absolutely true, so it's good to have it confirmed from you.
Stephen	I can imagine. He came very quietly, I think he had guessed that we suspected him of being a traitor for some time now.
Hugh	Which we had, hadn't we?
Stephen	Yes. When was it we first came to suspect him?
Hugh	Hoo, well I can't remember exactly, but it was certainly some time ago.
Stephen	Before last spring, I should think.
Hugh	Around there definitely. Certainly no later than the fourteenth of May, because that's my birthday and I remember saying that catching Costain and putting him out of harm's way would be the best Christmas present anyone could ever have.
Stephen	I remember you saying those exact words, Tony.
Hugh	But any old way, you managed to arrest him then?
Stephen	Yes. He was taken to the ninth floor and I had the job of interrogating him.
Hugh	That's never a pleasant task is it?
Stephen	It's one of the things I least enjoy having to do as a matter of fact Tony. It's very difficult when someone doesn't want to tell you things and you have to think up ways of *making* them tell you.
Hugh	Yes, that can call on all your know-how, can't it?
Stephen	Costain I'm afraid really didn't want to tell us anything. But I thought it would be much better if he did because if he's been working for the Russians for the last twenty years it's quite important that we know everything that he's been up to.

95

Hugh	That way we know which of our secrets have been given away and which ones are safe.
Stephen	That's exactly right.
Hugh	Is the Minister pleased that we've caught him at last?
Stephen	Well, while on the one hand Tony, he's delighted that Costain is behind bars, on the other hand he's extremely anxious to avoid any publicity. And on the other hand he's ...
Hugh	You've got three hands there, Control.
Stephen	Whoops, I wasn't counting very carefully, was I? Well, let's say he's also rather cross that we allowed a Soviet agent within our own ranks to go undetected for so long.
Hugh	A mixed reception then?
Stephen	I think that's a fair way of describing it, yes. So all in all it's been a pretty tiring forty-eight hours. Well, forty-four to be more accurate. But it seems like forty-eight, I can tell you. Well, forty-six or seven at least.
Hugh	Tell you what, Control – if you're feeling that tired, do you think a cup of coffee might perk you up?
Stephen	Oh I say, Tony, that's ever such a super thought. I'd just love one.
Hugh	Coming right up.
Stephen	You're a lifesaver, Tony and that's a fact.
Hugh	And I tell you what, Control ...
Stephen	Mm?
Hugh	I'm going to make it a good and strong one.
Stephen	Doh!

Puppy Appeal

Stephen sits behind a desk, addressing the camera.
There is an exceptionally cute puppy in his arms,
probably a golden labrador.

Stephen   This puppy, Snipper, is in most desperate need
of help. Four months ago Snipper's mother died,
and only three days later her father was killed
by a hit-and-run driver. Barely five months old
and an orphan, Snipper was also faced with the
embarrassing and painful affliction of incontinence.
It's a condition that we in the West don't talk
much about: shame keeps millions of sufferers
silent, but Snipper's incontinence was a source
of great distress to her and rather than come to
terms with it, she ran away, to London. It was
on the way to London that Snipper was assaulted
and abused by an older dog. You can imagine the
effect this would have on an innocent puppy bitch
like Snipper. She was totally confused, bewildered
and hurt. We think that it is around that time that
she was struck with traumatic amnesia, a total
loss of memory. This, apart from anything else,
made it very difficult for her to know where she
was and what she was doing. She drifted into a
life of scavenging and prostitution, selling her soft,
furry young body just in order to stay alive. That
was the life she was living when we at the ASTL
found her. We were able to give her food, warmth,
and more than that – love, the one thing that
has been denied her in her short and tragically
unhappy life.

Snipper is taking an interest in life now. Her
memory is slowly returning, which is how we've

been able to piece together the details of her life, and with luck she will be able to lead a normal, happy and fulfilled life. But there are thousands of Snippers in Britain and we desperately need your help to carry on the work we are doing. We are an entirely independent charity, we receive no government funding and rely on public generosity to keep us going. If you're the kind of person who would like to help a Snipper then please send your donation, however large, to me, Stephen Fry, care of the BBC, instead.

VOX
POP

Stephen   So I just told them to stuff it. But they said it had been dead too long.

Critics Two

Stephen and Hugh are in the swivel chairs again, being revolting.

Stephen Well of course what I found particularly disappointing was their choice of . . .

Hugh Did that work for you?

Stephen What?

Hugh Their choice of . . .

Stephen No it didn't. I felt it was a mistaken choice, a misguided choice, a badly chosen choice.

Hugh They could have chosen better?

Stephen I think so. And of course, if they had chosen better . . .

Hugh Which they didn't.

Stephen Well of course not. But if they had, their limitations would have . . .

Hugh I was going to ask you about that.

Stephen But you didn't.

Hugh I was going to.

Stephen Well then, yes. Just so limited, you see. And that was bound to limit them.

Hugh So they were limited by their own limitations?

Stephen Nicely put.

Hugh Thank you. That leads me on to another question. May I?

Stephen Of course.

Hugh   Thanks. I wonder, is there a sense in which you're not completely revolting?

Stephen No sense whatsoever. I've looked hard for a sense, but at the end of it all I've come up senseless.

Hugh   Does that I wonder tie in with . . .

Stephen Precisely my point. Could one say, from any critical standpoint yet devised, that you are any distance at all from being utterly repulsive?

Hugh   Ah. Now that's interesting.

Stephen Oh dear. Wasn't meant to be.

Hugh   Never mind. There'll be other opportunities I'm sure.

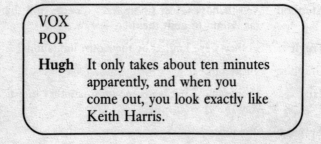

VOX
POP

Hugh   It only takes about ten minutes apparently, and when you come out, you look exactly like Keith Harris.

Sex Change

Hugh   *(To camera)* My guest tonight is someone who in
1987 caused a sensation by becoming the first
woman to undergo a complete and successful
sex change operation. In August of that year she
entered the Pert Frool clinic in Düsseldorf as
Melinda Coppice, author, broadcaster and mother
of three. Two weeks later she left that clinic as
Michael Coppice. His bestselling account of the
operation, the painful decisions leading up to it,
the painful incisions during the course of it and
the aftermath of fame that resulted from it have
made Michael Coppice a household name. Let's
meet him now – ladies and gentlemen, Michael
Coppice.

*Enter Deborah, completely normal woman. Shakes
hands with Hugh. They sit. The sofa they sit on is
dangerously soft and yielding: every now and then they
are out of physical control because it's so squashy and
hard to maintain balance in or on.*

Michael. Welcome.

Deborah   Thank you. Great pleasure.

Hugh   So. Michael. How would you say your life has
been since the operation?

Deborah   Well, I have to say firstly that everyone, my
family, my friends, the people I meet have been
enormously supportive since the operation that
transformed me into a man. Both my ex-husband
and my present wife have been tremendously
understanding.

Hugh   You now have a wife?

Deborah   Yes indeed. With two children.

Hugh	You are able to have children?
Deborah	Oh yes. I have fathered a wonderful pair of twins. It was a total gender change, the operation.
Hugh	And how successful would you say that operation has been?
Deborah	Well, you can see for yourself. One hundred per cent.
Hugh	Ye-e-es. How would you describe, as perhaps the only person in the world in a position to be able to do so, the difference between the sexes, then?
Deborah	In a way it's hard for me to answer that, Clive: you see although I have been completely transformed into a man, I am still a transvestite. Hence the women's clothes.
Hugh	You are still a transvestite?
Deborah	Yes. More properly a transexual. Rather a good one, I think you'll agree. You'd never know I was a man would you?
Hugh	No. No, I don't think I would. Does your wife object to your transexuality?
Deborah	She seems to understand and support me fully.
Hugh	Well let's meet her and find out. Ladies and gentlemen. Welcome now please Michael's wife Lucy Coppice.

Enter Stephen as manly as ever. Man's clothes.

Hugh	Welcome Lucy. *(They kiss)*
Stephen	Thank you. *(He squeezes Deborah's hand)*
Hugh	We were talking about whether or not you objected to the fact that your husband is a transexual.

102

Stephen   Oh good Lord no. I'm one myself.

Hugh   You are?

Stephen   Yes. It's my ambition some day to have an operation like Michael's and become a man.

Deborah   And I'm going to change myself back into a woman and we'll marry again.

Hugh   Are you worried that this might upset and confuse your children?

Stephen   Oh no, the twins are very aware of what's going on.

Hugh   Are they identical twins?

Deborah   That's right. A girl and a boy.

Hugh   Um – identical twins must surely be of the same sex . . . er . . .

Stephen   Yes, well Simon dresses as a girl and Lucy is a complete tomboy.

Hugh   But what sex were they originally?

Deborah   Um . . . ?

Stephen   Do you know, we can't remember.

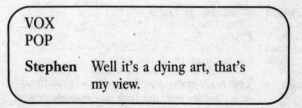

VOX
POP

Stephen   Well it's a dying art, that's my view.

Forward to the Past

Stephen answers the door to Hugh who is dressed in incredible futuristic gear.

Stephen Yes?

Hugh Hello, I come from the future.

Stephen *(Annoyed)* What?

Hugh I come from the future.

Stephen Do you? Do you, indeed?

Hugh That's substantially correct, yes. I come from a time in advance of your own.

Stephen Really?

Hugh Yes, really.

Stephen And what century exactly would you be from, I wonder?

Hugh I come from the twentieth century.

Stephen So not so significantly far advanced then?

Hugh Well, no. I come from a time five minutes ahead.

Stephen Five minutes.

Hugh Yes. Five of your primitive minutes. Goodbye.

Stephen What. You're going now?

Hugh Yes.

Stephen No message from the future?

Hugh There are laws, time laws we dare not interfere with, lest we meddle with our own destinies.

	Farewell. I may say I'm sorry that I can't return it. Please accept my apologies.
Stephen	Return what?
Hugh	What you lent me. It was burnt up in the time-leap. Still, as you rightly said, it was only Habitat anyway.

Exit Hugh.

| **Stephen** | *(Still standing in doorway)* Well, frankly. |

Enter Hugh wearing deerstalker and cape, looking very late Victorian.

Hugh	Good morning. If it is morning.
Stephen	You again.
Hugh	I don't think we've met.
Stephen	What?
Hugh	This is my first time in this neighbourhood.
Stephen	Oh don't be ridiculous, I was talking to you just five . . . minutes *(Voice trails off)* . . . ago.
Hugh	Something wrong?
Stephen	No, no. Probably just a day dream. How can I help you?
Hugh	Well the thing is, I'm a bit lost. I know this'll sound like the ravings of a complete imbecile, but you must believe me. I'm a time-traveller.
Stephen	Yes, yes. From the future.
Hugh	*(Puzzled)* No, from the past. Five minutes ago I projected myself five minutes into the future, into your time and I was wondering who is Prime Minister now?

Stephen	Margaret Thatcher. Look . . .
Hugh	Ah, really? Still? Some things never change. Has anyone invented a way of opening a packet of 'Hob Nob' biscuits without tearing their nails yet?
Stephen	No, look just what exactly –
Hugh	Is Noel Edmonds still alive?
Stephen	*(Surprised)* Not that I'm aware of. Look, is this some kind of practical joke?
Hugh	Well, I must go before I catch up with myself. I think next time I shall try going forward a bit. Farewell.

Exit Hugh.

Stephen	Bye then. This is getting very difficult to follow.

Enter Hugh dressed as normally as he ever is.

Hugh	Hello.
Stephen	And where are you from?
Hugh	This is going to sound quite unbelievable but I come from . . .
Stephen	. . . the funny farm.
Hugh	I'm sorry?
Stephen	Never mind, what time are you from then?
Hugh	North Finchley.
Stephen	What?
Hugh	North Finchley, call it Barnet.
Stephen	When?
Hugh	I'm sorry?
Stephen	When are you from?

Hugh	Are you alright?
Stephen	I – I think so, yes.
Hugh	I'm collecting.
Stephen	What?
Hugh	Collecting.
Stephen	What for?
Hugh	This blinkered, hidebound, reactionary government has no vision. I plan to build a machine. A machine that will enable man to travel . . .
Stephen	Through time, yes, yes, very clever.
Hugh	No. To travel to central London without getting caught in the traffic. The principle is simple: using ruthenium and polonium as energisers, I intend to build a prototype machine which will leap over traffic queues as if they weren't there. Simply key in the coordinates of the street you want and hey presto. Can I get a grant from the morons in government? No sir.
Stephen	You don't think there might be any unfortunate side-effects?
Hugh	What do you mean?
Stephen	Such as time-travel for instance.
Hugh	*(Laughing)* Oh I don't think so, you've been watching too many TV sketches.

Stephen looks into camera puzzled for the briefest of brief seconds.

Stephen	*(Tired)* Alright then, how much do you want?
Hugh	Oh, it's not money. It's just that the transducer needs a lampshade.
Stephen	What?

Hugh   I knew you'd think me crackpotted, but it's true. Just a simple common or garden lampshade, so that the gallium plate can reach P state in a picosecond and then instantly revert to an N state which . . .

Stephen   Yes, yes alright. I'll get you a lampshade. *(Goes in)*

Hugh   *(Calling after him)* Thank you! Thank you so much! You're a friend of science.

Stephen   *(Coming out with lampshade)* There you are.

Hugh   Marvellous. Bless you. I have the machine round the corner. It will only take five minutes to fit and then – London's traffic problem solved in a stroke.

Stephen   Right.

Hugh   I shall return your lampshade.

Stephen   Don't worry, it's only Habitat anyway . . . *(Voice trails away)*

Exit Hugh.

Stephen pauses for a while and then looks into camera.

I'm sure, logically, something weird should happen now, but I can't work out what.

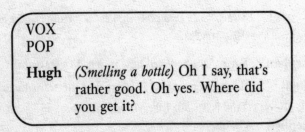

VOX
POP

Hugh   *(Smelling a bottle)* Oh I say, that's rather good. Oh yes. Where did you get it?

The Old Folks

Stephen is behind the reception desk of an old people's home. Hugh enters.

Hugh   Hello.

Stephen   You're not very old.

Hugh   Sorry?

Stephen   I say you're not very old.

Hugh   No, I . . .

Stephen   This is an old folks' home, you see, and consequently we do ask that people wishing to stay here are, at the very least, old. It's in our charter.

Hugh   I don't want to stay here.

Stephen   Oh. Then I must instantly demand that you pardon me. Have we been talking at cross purposes do you suppose?

Hugh   Possibly, yes.

Stephen   Whoops. My fault, quite dreadful of me. We'd better start again then.

Hugh   Right.

Stephen   Right.

Hugh   I wondered if . . .

Stephen   You're not very old.

Hugh   What?

Stephen   This is an old folks' home, you see, and consequently . . .

Hugh	No, I don't want to stay here. I've come to see my aunt.
Stephen	Oh. No. Oh no. What a shame. She died.
Hugh	Who did?
Stephen	Your aunt. If you'd only been a few hours earlier.
Hugh	Wait a minute. You don't know who I am yet.
Stephen	I don't have to. We only had one aunt, you see and she passed away last night. Oh, we shall miss her indeed. Her cheerfulness, her sense of fun . . .
Hugh	Hold on. Do you mind if we just check the name first, to make sure we're talking about the same person?
Stephen	If there's the slightest chance that it'll help you to confront some of the painful unanswered questions that must be weighing upon you at this most difficult of times, then all of a surely.
Hugh	Thank you.
Stephen	Please don't thank me, nephew.
Hugh	Wh . . . ?
Stephen	I do this job because I love it. How many people can say that? Less than a dozen I fancy rotten. Yes, here it is. Room 14, aunt, died at ten o'clock last night.
Hugh	Yes, what was her name?
Stephen	Fourteen.
Hugh	No, her name.
Stephen	Well now, I don't think we actually have a record of her name. There isn't much space on these cards, you see? I keep on saying to the Trustees – did I say 'saying'? Beseeching on bended legs, rather – 'give me bigger cards' but . . .

Hugh   What was her name?

Stephen   Well before you rush headlong down that tree-lined avenue, let me just say that we're very much given to using nicknames, here.

Hugh   Nicknames?

Stephen   Indeed, yes. To myself and the rest of the staff your aunt will always be remembered as 'fourteen'. Sounds a bit informal, I know. But that's our style here. We leave formality very much outside on the doorstep, together with a cheerful note to the milkman. From the day she arrived, 'fourteen' just seemed so right somehow.

Hugh   Are you saying that a woman died here last night and you don't even know her name?

Stephen   I know that it's hard sometimes for an outsider to enter a home like this, and it is a home – did I mention that? Did I make that abundant? – and straight away understand what it is we're really trying to do here.

Hugh   My aunt's name is Amanda Thighkiss.

Stephen   Well there you are, you see. Amanda Thighkiss. How could we have called her that? It's so cold, so unfriendly. And you can see how small the cards are. I'd be lucky to squeeze 'A. Thigh' on one of these.

Deborah, as a very old lady, appears next to Stephen.

Deborah   Please . . .

Stephen   Whoops! Hahaha . . .

Stephen tries to push Deborah's head down.

Deborah   Just a piece of bread, a biscuit, anything.

Hugh	Aunt Amanda?
Deborah	*(Popping up)* Neville! Oh thank God!
Hugh	Are you alright?
Stephen	*(Standing in front of her)* Oh dear. Oh dear, oh dear.
Hugh	What's the matter?
Deborah	I'm starving. Have you brought any food?
Stephen	Oh dear, oh dear, oh dear. I'll never forgive myself for this. You should have been spared this. I'd give anything for you to have been spared this.
Hugh	You told me she was dead.
Deborah	Who was dead?
Stephen	As if the shock of the news was not enough, you've now had to see this. I'm so sorry. So very sorry.
Hugh	What are you talking about?
Stephen	I'm sorry that you should be confronted with the body in this fashion. It's all very distressing.
Hugh	Body?
Stephen	Still, spiritually she's in a better place now. Let's be grateful for that.
Hugh	She's standing right there.
Stephen	Well of course her body is right here, but her soul . . . Who knows what beautiful journey . . . ?
Deborah	Please, Neville, have you got any food?
Hugh	Food? No. Are you hungry?
Deborah	I haven't eaten since lunchtime yesterday.
Hugh	Lunchtime yesterday? What's the matter, don't you feed people here at all?

Stephen	Of surely course.
Hugh	You do?
Stephen	Indeed yes. Our guests have had more hot dinners than you've had . . . than you've had.
Hugh	Then why hasn't my aunt been fed since yesterday?
Stephen	Ah. You're a stranger to death, I can see. Let me just say, as simply as I can, that it is deeply unusual to give food to dead people.
Hugh	What?
Stephen	Unless, of course, it is specified in the will. Otherwise we tend to look upon it as a needless extravagance. However, if it is your wish . . .
Hugh	What are you talking about? My aunt is not dead.
Stephen	Are you a medical person?
Hugh	No.
Stephen	Ah.
Hugh	Look, she's standing there, talking and breathing . . .
Deborah	*(Faintly)* Aaagh . . .
Hugh	. . . just . . . and you're telling me that she's dead.
Stephen	I can readily understand that the effect of the shock taken with the friendly brightness of our decor would make it hard for you to grasp . . .
Hugh	She is not dead. *(To Deborah)* Are you?
Deborah	No.
Hugh	There.
Stephen	Oh I know how much you want to believe it. Otherwise how could you stand the loss? But you

	see, I too have lost. When dear old fourteen died, a little part of me died with her.
Hugh	Did it?
Stephen	Yes, I shall be burying that little part of me this afternoon after a simple but affecting ceremony in the garden. Would you like to come?
Hugh	Look. Why do you keep saying that she's dead? Just tell me . . .
Stephen	Well, if it won't be too painful . . .
Hugh	No go on. I'm keen to know.
Stephen	Brave, brave nephew. What happened was this. I sent out a final reminder, thirty days after the last payment fell due, and believe me, even at that stage I still hoped that all might be well . . .
Hugh	Wait a minute. Payment for what?
Stephen	Why, room and board. Payment comes due on a monthly basis. Most of our guests favour an arrangement whereby . . .
Hugh	You mean she hasn't paid her bill?
Stephen	Sadly, no. We're all so very sorry. My deepest and most heartfelt condolences to you.
Hugh	How much?
Stephen	Your very pardon?
Hugh	How much does she owe?
Stephen	A very tragic one hundred and nineteen pounds and seven pence.
Hugh	*(Getting out cheque book)* Well for goodness sake, *(Writing)* one hundred . . . nineteen pounds and seven . . . pence. There.
Stephen	*(Taking it without looking – his gaze is fixed on Deborah, who has started to eat the desk blotter)*

114

Fourteen! Can it be true? Can I be believant of my eyes! I'm sure I saw . . . *(To Hugh, briskly)* Would you mind putting your card number on the back?

Hugh does so and hands over the cheque.

Yes! She moves, she stirs, she seems to feel the breath of life beneath her keel. It's a miracle! A miracle!

A porter enters wheeling a conspicuously dead person on a trolley.

Number twelve! Look at this! Number fourteen has come back to life! Oh wonder of wonders!

Hugh   Now come on, that woman really is dead.

Stephen   On the contrary, sir. She has a standing order.

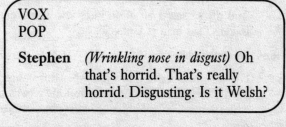

VOX
POP

Stephen   *(Wrinkling nose in disgust)* Oh that's horrid. That's really horrid. Disgusting. Is it Welsh?

Hugh's Brain

Enter Stephen, holding a human brain.

Stephen   Ladies and gentlemen, I wonder how many of you know what this is? Well most of you will know that it's a brain, a human brain, but can you guess whose brain it is? I should tell you first of all that for some time I've enjoyed a bit of a reputation as a practical joker, you see, and what I've done is this. While Hugh was asleep in his dressing room, I crept in and very carefully removed his brain, being sure not to wake him up. This is Hugh's brain. He'll be coming on in a second, let's see if he's noticed anything's amiss . . .

Enter Hugh, laughing cheerfully.

Hugh   Hahahaha.

Stephen   Hello, Hugh. What have you been up to?

Hugh   I've just been watching that Noël Edmonds show, it's so funny. Just brilliant. Completely brilliant.

Stephen   Ha. Are you feeling alright?

Hugh   Yeah, fine, fine.

Stephen   Good.

Hugh   And then I saw a bit of an interview with Kenneth Baker. That man is fantastic.

Stephen   Do you think so?

Hugh   Oh, he's wonderful. He's just what this country needs. He's firm, courageous, and his views on education are so enlightened, so sophisticated, so utterly enthralling. Well, he's an enthralling person, of course.

Stephen *(To audience)* It's great, isn't it? We can see the difference, but poor old Hugh hasn't noticed a thing. *(To Hugh)* D'you recognise this?

Hugh It's a cauliflower.

Stephen Hahaha. A cauliflower. Hasn't he been a sport, ladies and gentlemen? So what are you going to do now?

Hugh I thought I'd write a letter to 'Points of View'.

Stephen Dear oh dear oh dear. Perhaps I've gone a bit far.

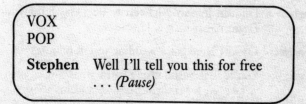

VOX
POP

Stephen Well I'll tell you this for free
. . . *(Pause)*

Christening

Mother (Deborah Norton) and father (Hugh) standing at font with baby. Stephen is the vicar. Hugh is very much the modern thrusting executive.

Stephen   I baptise thee Rupert Jeremy James –

Hugh   No, hold on a minute.

Stephen   What is it?

Hugh   You're right darling, Nicholas is better. Nicholas Thomas Geoffrey.

Stephen   Nicholas Thomas Geoffrey.

Deborah   You can't have Nicholas Thomas: that's a very ugly rhyme.

Hugh   You're right. What was the other one we liked?

Deborah   Timothy Nicholas Peter.

Hugh   No, Nicholas *Timothy* Peter.

Stephen   *(Dipping finger in water)* OK. Nicholas Timothy Peter?

Deborah   Yes.

Hugh   It's a shame to lose Jeremy though, isn't it?

Deborah   I still like Duncan.

Hugh   Duncan Jeremy Nicholas or Nicholas Jeremy Duncan?

Stephen   Look. I have got a wedding in ten minutes.

Hugh   You're being paid aren't you?

Stephen   *(Puzzled)* No . . .

Hugh	Nick's idea was Peregrine.

Hugh Nick's idea was Peregrine.

Deborah Oh darling, you can't call a baby Peregrine.

Stephen So Peregrine Jeremy Duncan . . .

Deborah I know it sounds silly but I've always loved Dick.

Stephen Erm . . .

Hugh Now Dirk's due for a revival.

Deborah Duncan Dirk Dick.

Hugh Rather fetching.

Stephen Duncan Dirk Dick, I baptise thee in the name of the Father and of the Son, and of the Holy Ghost, Amen. We receive this child into the congregation of Christ's flock and do sign him with the sign of the cross *(Signs with finger on forehead)* and in token that hereafter he shall not be ashamed to confess the faith of Christ crucified and manfully to fight under his banner against sin, the world and the devil, and to continue Christ's faithful soldier and servant unto his life's end. Amen.

Hugh No it's still not right . . . I don't know . . . hold on, what about Tweeble?

Deborah Oh darling . . .

Hugh Well it's our nickname for the little blighter anyway, so why not?

Deborah Tweeble Timothy James, I like it.

Hugh Yeah, Tweeble Timothy James.

Stephen I'm sorry, it's Duncan Dirk Dick, I've just done it.

Hugh Well, undo it.

Stephen Undo it?

Hugh	Yes.
Stephen	This is a Holy Sacrament of the Church, not a bleeding hotel reservation, you can't just undo it.
Hugh	You're beginning to annoy me, buster. Look at this card. *(Holds up white card)* What does this say?
Stephen	'Christening service'.
Hugh	Yes. Service, notice – not rudeness. It doesn't say 'Christening Rudeness'.
Stephen	I wasn't being rude.
Hugh	Just bear in mind that there are plenty of other religions you know. Some of them, I may say, offering much greater range and value.
Deborah	Not to mention carpets. Look at this.
Hugh	So come on. Hand him over.
Stephen	What?
Hugh	Hand him over. We'll take a look at the Mosque on Arlington Road, if it's all the same to you.
Stephen	But I haven't finished the service!
Hugh	The rudeness, you mean? Well you should have thought of that before.
Stephen	Look, you can't just walk out half way through. Think of the child!
Hugh	Screw the child. Haven't you heard the news?
Stephen	Well I've heard some news, but I doubt if it's the same news that you're . . .
Hugh	There's a revolution going on. Enterprise, initiative. Those who can't trim their fat go to the wall.
Stephen	What wall?
Hugh	What wa . . . ? You just don't know what I'm

talking about do you? I'm talking about the
way you're running this flea-bitten, one-horse
operation. Take this building. All this equity
tied up for what? A couple of weddings a week.
Pathetic. God, I'd like to get my hands on this
place. I could really do something. Shopping
arcade, four luxury flats, brasserie downstairs. It's
a criminal waste.

Stephen   *(Getting annoyed, puts baby in font to use both hands
to speak – no one notices)* Look, matey, this is a
church, not a dealing room. I am not interested
in your creepy theories about enterprise and
initiative. This place is founded on ideas a bit
more permanent than the Dow Jones Index.

Hugh   Yeah?

Stephen   Yeah. Something a tadge classier than 'buy long,
sell short and get into gilts'.

Hugh   Uhuh?

Stephen   The Church will be here long after your little brat
has grown up, ripped a few people off and died
unloved in his Spanish retirement villa.

Deborah   Portuguese, actually. And there's no need to be
so beastly.

Stephen   Well I'm sorry, but people like you really piss
me off.

Hugh   You've got a big mouth, mister. So what's your
pitch, your scam, your angle?

Stephen   Well look at you. You fight and deal and cheat
all your life to get enough money to spend a few
years wobbling your fat old bodies round a beach
or a golf course, but what provision have you
made for after your retirement?

Hugh   *After* my retirement?

Stephen   I'm talking about heaven.

Hugh	Heaven? Isn't that where the Gilroys went, darling?
Deborah	Devon.
Hugh	Oh yeah.
Stephen	After a hard life, don't you think you ought to treat yourself to a little long-term security? I'm talking about lifestyle, status, comfort, and peace-of-mind.
Deborah	*(Nudging Hugh)* Don't trust him, Pudding.
Hugh	Give me space, give me space.
Stephen	She's right, think about it, Pudding. Think about it. Talk to your independent spiritual adviser.
Hugh	Hmm. He may have something.
Stephen	And if you won't treat yourself, have a thought for Duncan Dirk Dick. Give him a chance to get in on the ground floor.
Hugh	Darling, and no disrespect to you, Vicar, but what I'm thinking is this. How about a mixed portfolio, whereby we spread him through Judaism, Islam, Hindu and so on, maintaining a firm base in the Church of England?
Deborah	It does sound safer.
Hugh	Exactly.
Stephen	Alright. So. Duncan Dirk Dick, I baptise thee in ...
Deborah	Well then it ought to be something like Duncan Isaac Sanji.
Hugh	Duncan Abraham Sanji would be nice.
Deborah	Or how about Duncan Abraham Naresh?
Stephen	Right. Do it yourselves. There's the water, there's the hymn book. I'm off for a slash.

Bank Loan

*Bank manager's office. Stephen sitting behind the desk.
Hugh enters, looking quite needlessly repellent, folders
and things tucked under his arm.*

Stephen   *(Rising)* Mr Lully?

Hugh   That's right. Glad you could see me at such
short notice.

Stephen   Not at all, come in, sit down. Coffee?

Hugh   Thank you.

Stephen   How do you like it?

Hugh   Decaffeinated, jug method, low mineral content
filtered spring water, not quite brought to the boil
with semi-skimmed milk and one Nutrasweet.
Unstirred.

Stephen   Right. *(Intercom)* Mark?

Voice   *(Intercom distort)* Yes.

Stephen   Do we still have that chemistry set in the office?

Voice   *(Intercom distort)* 'Fraid not.

Stephen   Right, one coffee then please.

Voice   *(Intercom distort)* K.

Stephen   So, Mr Lully, you'd like a loan?

Hugh   That's pretty much the size of it.

Stephen   You mention in your letter that you're starting
up a business and that you're interested in taking
advantage of our new 'Gredo' start-up package.

Hugh   That's correct.

Stephen   Yes, now first things first. What exactly is the product you're hoping to market?

Hugh   Ah, yes. Brought some samples along as a matter of fact.

Hugh gets out two small sachets.

Haven't actually settled on brand names yet. But there's basically two products. The blue sachet is cocaine and the red is heroin.

Stephen   I'm sorry?

Hugh   My own market research and some work undertaken by the packaging and graphics team has revealed that cocaine is thought of as a fresher, brighter product, hence the blue, and heroin is warmer and more passionate, therefore red. You disagree? I'd value your input.

Stephen   You're planning to distribute and sell drugs?

Hugh   On the button. The market's there, I'm ready to go, and let's face it – Europe's open for business.

Stephen   Ye-e-es.

Hugh   Problem?

Stephen   Possibly. Possibly.

Hugh   I know what you're going to say. It's a market that up until now has been hedged about with a lot of rules and regulations, and let me tell you this. When I first began to look at this market, I thought to myself, 'hey, I'd be better off manufacturing red tape'. Hahaha!

Stephen   Red tape, yes.

Hugh   But thank God, times are changing. Whole new markets are opening up, and I'm ready to play them.

Stephen	Right.
Hugh	The demand is there, no question.
Stephen	Uh huh.
Hugh	The most exciting thing for me is that it's such a young market.
Stephen	Really?
Hugh	Immensely young. Consumer profiling indicates the twelve to fifteen-year-old segment. And if we can instil in them product loyalty, that's got to be good news.
Stephen	Aha. But . . . but . . .
Hugh	I know what you're going to say. 'Do they have the income?' right? Well, what I always say is, 'if the product's right, they'll find the income.' Their mothers' handbags, car stereos, old age pensioners, wherever.
Stephen	Mmm. I meant, well . . . I hesitate to use a word like this. I know it's old-fashioned. But do you think it's strictly moral?
Hugh	I beg your pardon?
Stephen	Is it moral?
Hugh	Moral?
Stephen	Yes.
Hugh	I'm not sure if I've actually got any precise figures on that . . .
Stephen	Yes, I actually mean . . . is it moral to do this at all? You know . . . children and so on.
Hugh	Well. Let me turn the question round and ask you this. Would you rather we stood by and watched the Germans, the Dutch, the South Americans take our market share? Where's your precious morality then?

Stephen Well ...

Hugh Up a gum tree without a paddle, that's where it is. The question is this. Either you believe in market forces or you don't.

Stephen Well actually, I'm afraid to say I don't.

Hugh You don't?

Stephen No. I used to of course, when I was a child, but like everyone else, I discovered as I grew older that it was all made up.

Hugh Made up?

Stephen Yes. I can still remember the exact moment. It was Christmas Eve. I can't have been more than about thirty years old. I couldn't sleep, so I crept downstairs and heard my parents laughing about market forces, and saying that they'd have to break it to me sooner or later. Bit of a blow, I can tell you. And then two years after that, I discovered there was no such thing as Father Christmas either.

Hugh You're kidding?

Stephen Oh sorry, did you ... ?

Hugh Yes I did. Tscch.

Stephen Oh dear.

Hugh Growing up, eh?

VOX
POP

Stephen   Well, you haven't paid
me yet.

Ignorance

Stephen and Hugh are having a chat in a setting yet to be decided.

Stephen   Interested in politics at all?

Hugh   Interested?

Stephen   Yes.

Hugh   It's my hobby.

Stephen   Is it?

Hugh   Crikey yes. Politics? Oh yes. Of course it's mostly a weekend thing I'm afraid, but come Sunday, it's down the end of the garden and politics, politics, politics. In answer to your question, yes. I'm a bugger for politics.

Stephen   What do you think of Nigel Lawson?

Hugh   Nigel . . .

Stephen   Lawson.

Hugh   Lawson, yes. *(Long pause)* What d'you think of him?

Stephen   He's a twerp.

Hugh   Oh, thank God for that. I thought he might have been a friend of yours or something. Yes, he's a twerp. What a twerp. Tscch.

Stephen   At least you know who he is.

Hugh   I don't actually, to be honest.

Stephen   You don't?

Hugh   Not who he is, no. I've always just thought of him

	as a twerp. Never bothered to look any deeper than that. It's the shortage of time . . .
Stephen	He's Chancellor of the Exchequer. Just.
Hugh	No. Is he? The old bastard. Nigel Lawson, the Chancellor of the Exchequer? What a twerp. Tscch.
Stephen	*(To camera)* Perhaps you can see what we're trying to do here. Hugh is trying to act the part of a man who doesn't know very much about politics. *(To Hugh)* What do you think of Douglas Hurd?
Hugh	Douglas Hurd. Er . . . Pretty lukewarm about him, to be honest.
Stephen	Really?
Hugh	Yeah. Bit of a twerp. But . . .
Stephen	*(To camera)* Hugh is pretending not to know who Douglas Hurd is.
Hugh	. . . you know, it takes all sorts to make a world.
Stephen	D'you think?
Hugh	Oh definitely.
Stephen	You don't think that with fewer twerps, you could make a better world?
Hugh	Oh you've got to keep the number of twerps down, yes. You can't let them run out of control.
Stephen	Tell me something. Did you vote at the last election?
Hugh	Oh they haven't banned them as well, have they?
Stephen	What?
Hugh	Was that the last election? Never going to be any more, ever again? Tscch! And I missed it.
Stephen	*(To camera)* I suppose what we're trying to say

with this sketch is, can democracy really work
as long as the people who vote are kept, or keep
themselves, in ignorance of political affairs?

Hugh Is that what we're trying to say?

Stephen Yes.

Hugh Blimey.

Stephen Because let's face it, doesn't the constitution of
the present government show, more clearly than
a thousand pictures ever could, that the people of
this country haven't the faintest idea who they're
voting for?

Hugh Are we trying to say that as well, with this sketch?

Stephen Oh yes.

Hugh Turning out to be quite an ambitious sketch, then?

Stephen You've got to aim high in my view. So, you don't
really know anything about Nigel Lawson or
Douglas Hurd?

Hugh No.

Stephen So I think this has gone some way towards
proving . . .

Hugh Mind you, I don't see why I should.

Stephen Pardon?

Hugh They don't know anything about me. Do they?

Stephen Well . . .

Hugh I mean, you say I don't know anything about
them, so how can I vote, but I say they don't know
anything about me, so how can they vote . . . to
make laws about me?

Stephen Mmm. That would be quite a good point, if it
weren't so pathetic.

Hugh   Oh I see. We're not aiming that high, then? We don't want to say too much with this sketch?

Stephen   No.

Hugh   But there's so much more we could say.

Stephen   Perhaps, but I'm afraid that time, the old enemy has beaten us again, and we can only say that the pen of my aunt is bigger than the patio of my uncle.

Hugh   Huh. Quite a pen.

Stephen   Quite an aunt.

VOX
POP

Stephen   On the bottom. Right on the bottom. Saying 'Made In Korea'. I don't know what made him say that.

A Bit of a Pain in the Bottom

Stephen enters a surgery. Hugh is sitting behind a desk.

Stephen Hello, Doctor.

Hugh Ah, come in. Look, you're the last, do you mind if this is very quick?

Stephen Er . . . no.

Hugh Alright then, how can I help?

Stephen *(Very fast)* Well Doctor, the fact is that I've got a bit of a pain in the bottom.

Hugh *(Just as fast, if not faster)* A bit of a pain in the bottom, I see. How did this happen?

Stephen Well I was out shopping this afternoon, and across the other side of the road a bomb went off in a shop.

Hugh A bomb? Good heavens!

Stephen Yes, and anyway, the whole pane of glass in the window of the shop next to me blew out.

Hugh The whole pane?

Stephen Yes, and anyway, a bit of the pane flew out and hit me in the arm.

Hugh The arm.

Stephen Yes. So I dropped my shopping, unfortunately on the foot of a horse that was standing in the street.

Hugh A horse?

Stephen Yes. A Horse. Are you deaf? And the horse shied and just as I was bending down to pick up my shopping this horse kicked me in the other arm.

131

Hugh   The other arm? I see.

Stephen   So I went over to a doorway and sat down. But I didn't look where I was sitting, there was glass everywhere, and as I sat down I got a bit of glass right in the palm of my hand.

Hugh   Palm of your hand?

Stephen   Yes and I had this bottle of strong acid in my bag and unbeknownst to me I spilt some on the step when I stood up, sharply, from the pain of the bit of pane of glass in the palm of my hand.

Hugh   I see, you spilt some acid.

Stephen   So then I caught the bus home.

Hugh   You caught the bus home.

Stephen   Yes, you are deaf. And on the bus I sat next to this pervert. He took out an enormous carrot, and at knife point he . . .

Hugh   Good Lord.

Stephen   He made me put it up my nose, while he watched.

Hugh   Heavens.

Stephen   So I ran out of the bus, which was moving, so I landed with a great bump and grazed my knee. But eventually I got home.

Hugh   Good.

Stephen   And I rushed to the bathroom because I was dying to go, you know . . .

Hugh   Mmm.

Stephen   But I rushed out of the bathroom, because there's no toilet in there, and I went into the lavatory instead. But there wasn't any paper.

Hugh   Ah!

Stephen   So I had to get some from the cupboard. I then went upstairs to change, and there was a wasp in my new pair of trousers.

Hugh   Oh, a wasp!

Stephen   Yes, so I killed it. Then I went downstairs and watched television.

Hugh   Mmm.

Stephen   And it was that Paul Daniels, who's a bit of a pain in the bottom. Doctor, what can you do about it?

Hugh   Doh!

Stephen   Doh!

Both   Doh!!!

VOX
POP

Stephen   I said to him, he must have been about fourteen, then. I said 'Son, you can't carry on forever just hanging onto your mother's apron. She's going to want it back one day.'

Inspector Venice

A woman answers the door. Hugh is standing there, in a raincoat and pork pie hat.

Hugh Good evening, Chief Inspector Venice, Burnham CID. May I come in?

Woman Of course you can, dear. It's your house.

She turns and walks away, leaving the door open.

Hugh You stupid woman! You stupid bloody woman! Come back here! Are you mad? I could be anybody! I could be a maniac!

Woman You're my husband, dear.

Hugh How do you know that? I mean how do you know that? Have I produced any identification?

Woman No.

Hugh No, exactly.

Woman But . . .

Hugh Ask to see my warrant card.

Woman *(Sighs)* Can I see your warrant card, dear?

Hugh Certainly madam. A very wise precaution, if I may say so.

Hugh produces warrant card, and holds it under her nose.

Woman Good, now do you . . .

Hugh Well look at it! You haven't even looked at it! Jesus, I could have bought this in Whitechapel,

134

	for all you know. I could be a maniac with a fake warrant card.
Woman	Alright. 'Chief Inspector . . .
Hugh	Don't leave the door open! God almighty! Use the chain, woman! What do you think it's there for?

She closes door. Hugh stays outside while she reads the card.

Woman	*(Off)* 'Chief Inspector Venice, Burnham CID.'

She opens the door again.

	Now come in and have your dinner, dear.
Hugh	Come in where?
Woman	The kitchen.
Hugh	I'm sorry. I have no authorisation to enter the kitchen.
Woman	You don't need it. It's your kitchen.
Hugh	Our kitchen, dear.
Woman	Our kitchen.
Hugh	You know perfectly well, I cannot enter our kitchen without your special permission.
Woman	You have my permission.
Hugh	Haven't you forgotten something, dear?
Woman	What?
Hugh	We agreed that we would both get telephone confirmation of the other's identity, before either of us gave special permission.
Woman	Oh Christ.
Hugh	Here's the telephone, dear. And remember. Better

safe than cut up into tiny pieces by a maniac pretending to be me.

She dials.

Woman   Burnham CID? Have you got an Inspector Venice in your department? *(Pause)* Thank you very much indeed.

Hugh   Well?

Woman   They've never heard of you.

Hugh   Damn. Anyway, what's for supper? Smells great.

Woman   They've never heard of Inspector Venice.

Hugh   Probably just a joke. We're always having jokes, down the station.

Woman   You're not a policeman, are you?

Hugh   No. No, I'm not.

Woman   What are you?

Hugh   A maniac.

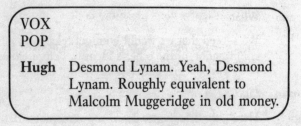

VOX POP

Hugh   Desmond Lynam. Yeah, Desmond Lynam. Roughly equivalent to Malcolm Muggeridge in old money.

Special Squad

Deborah is sitting on a sofa watching television.
Suddenly there is some extremely violent hammering at
the door. We hear Stephen and Hugh off.

Stephen   *(Off)* Just turn the handle.

More crashing.

(Off) Turn the handle. What's the matter
with you?

Hugh   *(Off)* Nothing.

More crashing.

Stephen   *(Off)* All you've got to do is . . .

Hugh   *(Off)* Look, I've carried this bloody thing all the
way from the car park, I'm not going to just turn
the handle and walk in.

Stephen   *(Off)* All right, well I'll turn the handle.

Hugh   *(Off)* Do what you like. I'm smashing this bloody
door in.

The door opens. Stephen enters the room.

(Off) Close the door, close the door.

Hugh stays in the doorway and smashes the door to
pieces with a sledgehammer.

Deborah   *(Scared)* What do you want?

Stephen   Mrs Catherine Popey?

Deborah Yes? What? Who are you?

Stephen Sorry to disturb you madam, my colleague and I are making some routine door-to-door enquiries in this area. D'you mind if we come in?

The door is finally off its hinges.

Hugh Finished.

Deborah Well, why didn't you ring the bell?

Stephen You see, I knew this would happen. She's now asking why we didn't ring the bell.

Hugh We thought you were out.

Stephen No, that's the wrong answer. That's the wrong answer.

Hugh We didn't want to disturb you.

Stephen No. No no no.

Hugh If we had rung the bell, there would have been no point in my having carried a sledgehammer all the way from the car park.

Deborah I see.

Stephen *(Pause)* Yup. Looks like we may have got away with that one. Now Mrs Popey, is your husband at home?

Deborah What?

Stephen Your husband. Is he at home at the current time?

Deborah I haven't got a husband.

Stephen You haven't got a husband? I see. Right.

Hugh Well when do you expect him back?

Deborah What?

Stephen No. No. That's the wrong question.

138

Hugh	Is it?
Stephen	Yes it is. Now then . . .
Hugh	When do you expect her back?
Stephen	Now then Mrs Popey, please excuse the incompleteness of our records. Computer trace indicates that you are currently the holder of a husband.
Deborah	Well I'm not.
Stephen	You're not. Well I'll have my colleagues amend the record accordingly. Now then Mrs Popey.
Deborah	Yes?
Stephen	Your husband's been a bit busy lately, hasn't he?
Deborah	What?
Stephen	Been giving us the proper runaround.
Hugh	He's scum. That's what he is. He's a scumbag. A great big bag of scum, he is, scumming around in a big bag. That's what he is. And he always will be.
Deborah	I haven't got a husband. I'm not married.
Hugh	You can take the scum out of the bag, but you can't take the bag out of the scum.
Stephen	Yeah . . .
Hugh	Boil in the bag scum, that's what he is.
Stephen	Yeah, my colleague has perhaps adopted a rather more forthright tone than I would have chosen, but then I like to think that's why we work so well together. Because we compliment each other, you see.
Deborah	Really?
Stephen	Yes, we compliment each other beautifully. Watch this. You're looking very smart today.

Hugh	Thank you. That's a very nice haircut.
Stephen	You see? Teamwork. Now then. To business, Mrs Popey. Your husband has . . .
Deborah	For heaven's sake. How many times do I have to tell you? I haven't got a husband.
Stephen	Well now . . .
Hugh	Twenty-five.
Stephen	Excuse me for just a moment, would you, Mrs Popey? *(To Hugh)* What?
Hugh	She's got to tell us twenty-five times that she hasn't got a husband.
Stephen	Why?
Hugh	Once for every day in the week.
Stephen	Yeah, that doesn't quite work.
Hugh	Doesn't it?
Stephen	No.
Hugh	Alright. Once for every year he's going to spend inside. The scumbag.
Deborah	Look, I don't know who you are, or why you want to speak to a husband I haven't got, but I'm telling you . . .
Stephen	Oh, we don't want to speak to him.
Deborah	Don't you?
Stephen	No no no.
Hugh	No no. Speak to him? No.
Stephen	If I may say so, I think you've been watching too many films, Mrs Popey.
Deborah	Well whatever. The point is, I haven't got a husband and therefore do you think it's possible that you might actually have the wrong house?

Stephen	No no no.
Hugh	No no no no no no no.
Stephen	No.
Hugh	No. You see, we've already been there.
Deborah	Where?
Hugh	To the wrong house. We've just come from the wrong house, just now.
Stephen	My colleague is absolutely right, as it happens Mrs Popey. We have, just this minute, come from the wrong house. So that argument doesn't really stand up, I'm afraid.
Hugh	No. That argument falls straight over.
Stephen	Yeah.
Hugh	And just lies there.
Stephen	Now since you claim to be alone in the house, you won't mind us having a quick look around?
Deborah	How quick?
Stephen	Very quick.
Deborah	Help yourself.
Stephen	Thank you.

Stephen and Hugh wave their heads about, stupidly.

There. That didn't hurt, did it?

Hugh	It did actually.
Deborah	Just whatever you do, don't wake up my son.
Stephen	I beg your pardon?
Hugh	Yeah so do I. I beg it as well.
Deborah	My son is asleep upstairs. I'd rather you didn't wake him.

Stephen	Now wait a minute Mrs Popey. Wait just a minute.
Hugh	Whoah there, boy! Whoah!
Stephen	Hold on one second. You have a son?
Deborah	Yes.
Stephen	Well now Mrs Popey, we may be stupid, but we're not clever. How do you come to have a son without having a husband? That sounds mightily ingenious.
Deborah	He was a sailor.
Stephen	Mmm. In the Navy?
Deborah	No, with the Nat West.
Stephen	I see. Well, we'll leave that for the moment. This son of yours, he's upstairs, you say?
Deborah	Yes, asleep.
Hugh	What, tired, is he?
Stephen	I'm not surprised he's tired after the merry dance he's been leading us.
Hugh	Yes, a very merry dance indeed he's been a-leading us of. Highly merry. Ha, ha, ha, it's so merry.
Stephen	I think we'd better have a word with this son of yours, Mrs Popey, if it's all the same to you.
Deborah	Only if you promise to leave as soon as you've finished.
Stephen	Of course Mrs Popey. We'll leave just as soon as we've finished being here.

Deborah exits.

	What a charming woman.
Hugh	Charming. Delightful. A really super woman.

142

Stephen	She's taken it so well.
Hugh	This is it, you see.
Stephen	Too well, perhaps.
Hugh	Well I didn't want to say, but yes, she may have taken it too well.

Deborah reenters, carrying a cot containing a small baby.

Deborah	This is my son William.
Stephen	Aha. You've been a bit of a naughty boy, haven't you, William?
Hugh	Ask him what he's done with the stuff.
Stephen	Now then William, what have you done with the stuff? *(To Hugh)* What stuff?
Hugh	I don't know. It was a trap.
Stephen	He hasn't fallen for it.
Hugh	*(Pause)* Scumbag.

> VOX
> POP
>
> **Hugh** Who are the great hat-wearers of
> today? There aren't any, you see.
> No one for the kids to look up to.

Orthodoxy

Headmaster's study. Stephen is behind a desk. Quite a public-schooly sort of study, but not overdone. Not actually window seats and old English Gothic windows, but quite cosy nonetheless. Enter Hugh dressed as a schoolboy. Grey uniform, darkish tie. Dull appearance.

Stephen   Ah, Bamford, come in, come in.

Hugh   Thank you, sir.

Stephen   So, Bamford. First day at St Gray's, eh?

Hugh   Yes, sir.

Stephen   Getting on alright?

Hugh   *(Shy)* Not too bad thank you, sir.

Stephen   Not too bad thank you, sir. Not too bad thank you, sir. Good, good. Good, good, good. You'll find it strange at first I dare say.

Hugh   It's a bit hard to find my feet, sir, yes.

Stephen   Really, well we'll have to do something about that. Some sort of name-tape sewn into them may help. But the first few days are always a little bewildering.

Hugh   Yes sir.

Stephen   Mind you Bamford, if you were to believe everything you read on the television you'd think new boys spent their days being roasted in front of fires and having dessert fruits pushed up their . . . their . . . there couldn't be less truth in that, could there, Bamford?

Hugh   No, sir.

Stephen	No, sir. Quite right. Schools like ours have survived because they've moved into the modern age, Bamford. Progress, Bamford.
Hugh	Sir.
Stephen	Progress isn't a dirty word, you know. Arse is a dirty word, and so, to some extent, is labia. Learn that, Bamford, learn and obey.
Hugh	Yes, sir. I will.
Stephen	But progress is the towel that rubs us dry. Each soft cotton flick of progress can penetrate the darkest, dampest corners of our mired and filthy selves, and polish us clean.
Hugh	I didn't know that, sir.
Stephen	Well Bamford, now you do, now you do. Good. Oh good. First class. Fine. Splendid. Sp-len-did. Excellent. Eccellente.
Hugh	Um, was there anything else?
Stephen	Hm? Yes, yes indeed there was anything else. There's a rumour going around the Lower Fourth that you have an uncle who is a Member of Parliament.
Hugh	Yes, sir.
Stephen	A Labour Member of Parliament, Bamford.
Hugh	Sir.
Stephen	Now, on the whole, boys are a pretty healthy, tolerant and forgiving lot, Bamford. But they can be cruel. You can answer this next question with perfect frankness, it won't transgress that schoolboy code we masters know and respect so well. Have you been teased at all about this unfortunate relationship?
Hugh	Well sir, not teased exactly . . . more, well, beaten up.

Stephen	I see. I'm sorry you saw fit to sneak on your schoolmates, Bamford. That disappoints me. I shall overlook it this time.
Hugh	Thank you, sir.
Stephen	You're a new bug after all. Do you know why they have been ballyragging you?
Hugh	I must say, I'm a bit puzzled by it, to be frank, sir.
Stephen	Well, you see, in my history and general study lessons I sometimes speak about Socialism and I expect that's made something of an impression on your classmates. Their political zeal may have got the better of them.
Hugh	Oh.
Stephen	You see, I tell the boys, Bamford, and this may come as quite a shock to you, that while socialism is all very well in practice it doesn't work in theory.
Hugh	I didn't know that, sir.
Stephen	Yes. Quite a thought isn't it?
Hugh	And that's why they punch me in the face a lot, is it sir?
Stephen	Well Bamford, they know that the real evil of socialism lies in its treatment of people as units. It discounts the individual, Bamford. It's the grey, dull uniformity of it all.
Hugh	Yes, sir.
Stephen	And the – have you got your top button undone, Bamford?
Hugh	Oh, yes, sir.
Stephen	(As if reciting a catechism) 'The top button to be done up only on Crimson Days or on the Thursday preceding exeats, otherwise the middle button unless you have a note from matron to say

146

you have a veruka in which case the bottom button may be done up, but only if the left sock is rolled halfway down between patella and Achilles tendon on a line previously drawn by Mr de Vere.'

Hugh   Sorry, sir, I forgot.

Stephen   Alright. Don't let it happen again. Where was I?

Hugh   Grey dull uniformity of it all, sir.

Stephen   Yes. Yes, exactly. Regimented lines of soulless automata, putting state before self, sacrificing everything for 'the good of the state' – it's a nightmare. That's the drawback of socialism, it discounts the – the what, boy?

Hugh   The person, sir?

Stephen   No, the individual! Get it right. The individual is paramount in any political system – your hair is two thirds of an inch over the collar, see Mr Buttaris for a licking – individualism is all. Alright, Bamford. That's all. We shall all make a mighty effort to overlook your uncle for the moment.

Hugh   Thank you sir.

Stephen   Good. And cheer up, eh? I know you'll do your best, what?

Hugh   I'll try, sir.

Stephen   That's right, boy. For the good of the school, eh? For the good of the dear old school. After all, we can point with pride at our history as the finest comprehensive in Durham, can't have you letting the side down. Off you go.

Hugh   Thank you, sir.

Stephen   *(Getting cane out of drawer)* And send Scargill minor in, would you?

Critics Three

Stephen and Hugh are in the swivel chairs again.

Stephen   Simon Clituris, you saw that. Thoughts? Inferences?

Hugh   Well, you see they fell into the old trap, the old trap of doing material that is essentially self-referential.

Stephen   By using the term 'self-referential', you mean . . . ?

Hugh   I mean to present myself as an impressive, even perhaps interesting, person.

Stephen   Ng. Ng. Aren't you getting a little tired though of humouresque material on television that is *about* television?

Hugh   Very tired. Exhausted.

Stephen   I think there's something very incestuous about people who make love to close blood relations. Perhaps it's just me.

Hugh   You see I wish, I wish they'd come to me when they first wrote that sketch. I could have just pointed out to them where they had gone wrong.

Stephen   This was my feeling exactly. Just nudged them gently in the right direction. It's all they needed. There's *some* talent there.

Hugh   Would you have said that?

Stephen   Well, not talent perhaps. I don't think they'd make very impressive critics for example.

Hugh   They always put out these things without consulting us first. I mean we're here to help.

Stephen   To help and to criticize. I'm sick up to the back stomach with the kind of comedy that has such utter and profound contempt for people like us.

Hugh   You see it's interesting isn't it, if you compare that sketch with the work of someone like Diana Suckleigh.

Stephen   Ah. Now, you see?

Hugh   Diana is observant, she's real, she's truthful.

Stephen   Always truthful. Very beautifully truthful and real. Very actual.

Hugh   I mean it doesn't all work.

Stephen   Oh no.

Hugh   She makes mistakes, but then which of them doesn't?

Stephen   That's right. We can't all be critics, for goodness' sake.

VOX
POP

Stephen   What you've got to do is boil them, for about ten or twelve minutes, and then slice them down the middle. But these judges nowadays are soft. Far too soft.

Spies Four

The spies' office. Stephen is pacing up and down frantically.

Hugh enters.

Hugh   Hullo there Control. Something up?

Stephen *(Still walking)* Well, it's a strange thing, Tony, but I've been advised that in order to stay fit I have to walk at least ten miles a day.

Hugh   But you've always been as fit as a flea, Control. Or a fiddle anyway. 'One of the fittest men in the service' you've been occasionally referred to as.

Stephen Look at this.

Stephen brings out a pedometer.

Hugh   What is it?

Stephen That's what I asked myself when the doctor gave it to me. It's a pedometer.

Hugh   A pedometer?

Stephen Yes, it measures how many miles I walk. Mrs Control is jolly careful to make sure that I put it on every morning, worst luck.

Hugh   Hah. Still, I'm sure Mrs Control has your best interests at heart.

Stephen Yes, that's true. Selfish of me to grumble. After all Tony . . .

Hugh   Yes?

Stephen It's for my good she's being quite so firm about it.

Hugh That's right.

Stephen Any golly way, you don't want to listen to my woes I dare say, Tony.

Hugh Oh, I don't know, they're quite interesting.

Stephen What brings you to the seventh floor this morning?

Hugh Well, do you remember the Minister asking us to jolly well hurry up and find out who was behind all these bombs that have been going off in government departments of lately?

Stephen Do I remember, Tony. Yes indeed, I most certainly do. A top priority investigation was demanded as I remember. Surveillance, tailing, tapping, no limit to the budget. 'Let's pull out all the stops on this one, Control, if you'd be kind enough', he said.

Hugh That's right. Quite a to-do.

Stephen I was going to ask you Tony. I put you in charge of that operation, have you come up with anything yet that might be a useful lead, or better still concrete information that could lead to some arrests?

Hugh Well, that's the very reason I popped in and surprised you at your walking, Control, I've just had a report from Commander Henderson of Special Branch.

Stephen That's the Scotland Yard branch founded earlier this century to deal with subversion and counter-insurgency?

Hugh That's the exact one.

Stephen I imagined quite strongly that it would be.

Hugh Yes. And they say that with some of our agents working undercover alongside them, they've arrested a cell of men and women who they believe they can prove are definitely responsible for the whole sorry wave of unfortunate and exasperating bomb attacks.

Stephen It was a sorry wave wasn't it?

Hugh It certainly was.

Stephen Well that is good news I must say.

Hugh I thought you'd be pleased.

Stephen I'm most pleased Tony. Well done. Full marks.

Hugh Calls for a coffee wouldn't you say?

Stephen It most certainly does.

Hugh I'll fetch you one.

Stephen No, Tony. It's my turn to fetch *you* one.

Hugh Well goodness, thank you Control.

Stephen No Tony, thank *you*. White no sugar, I think it is.

Hugh Yes please. This really is excessively kind of you Control.

Stephen Oh please don't mention it, Tony. Besides . . . *(patting his pedometer)* . . . the extra walk will impress Mrs Control!

Hugh Oh you.

Stephen Back in a mo, Tony.

Hugh Righto Control. I don't mind the wait.

> VOX
> POP
>
> **Hugh** No it would not be nice. It wouldn't be nice if all towns were like *any* town, let alone Milton Keynes.

Hugh's Poem

Hugh is reading a poem.

Hugh   Underneath the bellied skies,
Where dust and rain find space to fall,
To fall and lie and change again,
Without a care or mind at all
For art and life and things above;

In that, there, look just there,
No right left up down past or future,
We have but ourselves to fear.

Stephen   Hugh, you chose that poem. For God's sake why?

Hugh   I chose it for a number of reasons, Stephen.

Stephen   I see. The most important one being . . . ?

Hugh   Can I perhaps turn that question round and say 'because it was short'.

Stephen   The poem?

Hugh   That's right. I chose that poem because it was short.

Stephen   And that's significant?

Hugh   Well of course. With the pace of modern life being what it is, it seemed to me that most people just haven't got the time to spend on long poems, and this would therefore ideally suit the short-haul commuter or the busy housewife. This is a poem that can fit neatly into the most hectic of schedules, and leave time for other sporting or leisure activities.

Stephen   So that represents quite a boon to the modern poetry reader?

Hugh   Oh an enormous boon.

Stephen	Well of course we're always on the lookout for enormous boons. And I presume it's reasonably safe?
Hugh	Absolutely safe. This is a poem you could leave around the house in absolute confidence.
Stephen	Excellent. Presumably though, there must be shorter poems than that one?
Hugh	Oh good heavens yes.
Stephen	Good heavens yes?
Hugh	Good heavens yes. There's a poem by Richard Maddox called 'Institutions' that I can read for you now, if you like?
Stephen	Please.
Hugh	Here it is. 'Li.'
Stephen	That is short.
Hugh	It's very short indeed.
Stephen	Too short perhaps?
Hugh	Possibly.
Stephen	But I suppose that might just suit the busy senior executive who can only snatch a moment between meetings, and so on?
Hugh	Well that's right. That's certainly the market that Maddox was aiming for.
Stephen	Now at about this time, many people are going to be thinking about their summer holidays. Are there any poems that you might recommend to a family going on, say, a two-week get-away day leisure bargain break weekend away leisure holiday-break?
Hugh	Well first of all, let me give a warning to any families planning to take poetry on holiday with them.
Stephen	And that is?

Hugh	Be careful.
Stephen	Sounds like good advice to me.
Hugh	Check with your travel agent to see if there are any specific customs regulations regarding poetry, and if you're travelling outside the EEC, wrap up warm.
Stephen	Any particular advice on how to carry poetry, when travelling abroad?
Hugh	Yes, I would say it's definitely worth getting a proper travelling poetry bag.
Stephen	A travelling poetry bag?
Hugh	Yes. You can buy one of these at most big High Street travelling poetry bag shops.
Stephen	Great. Now I think you've got one last poem for us, before you go?
Hugh	I certainly have. This is 'The Rest of My Life' by R.P. Mitchell.
Stephen	*The* R.P. Mitchell?
Hugh	No. *A* R.P. Mitchell.
Stephen	Right.
Hugh	This poem is fairly solid, but at the same time, not too heavy. I think it's quite stylish.
Stephen	So it might suit, say, a young couple starting out in the catering business?
Hugh	If you like. 'Forward and back, Said the old man in the dance, As he whittled away at his stick, Long gone, long gone, Without a glance, To the entrance made of brick.'
Stephen	Thanks very much.

A Frank Talk

Stephen is getting out a couple of glasses and a bottle of whisky in the kitchen of his house. Hugh is sitting at the table looking faintly embarrassed.

Stephen   We'll wait for the ladies to get back from the theatre shall we?

Hugh   Yes, yes – good idea.

Stephen   I don't know what they see in it myself. Sitting there in the dark watching a lot of old nonsense.

Hugh   Oh well, they seem to enjoy it.

Stephen   I don't know about you, but I go to the theatre to be entertained.

Hugh   Well, I think they do too.

Stephen   If I want to see a lot of swearing and pretentious drivel I can stay at home.

Hugh   Still, anyway. They've been looking forward to it for a long time.

Stephen   *(Pouring out the drinks)* Right. Right.

Hugh   *I've* been looking forward to *this*, as a matter of fact, Matthew: this opportunity for a frank talk.

Stephen   Yes. Good. It's always nice to have a good – water?

Hugh   Thanks.

Stephen   *(Adding water to Hugh's drink)* – chat, isn't it?

Hugh   Mm. How long have I known you and Sarah now?

Stephen   Hoo, ch. What, must be nigh on.

Hugh   More I should think.

Stephen	Right. Possibly even more.
Hugh	You and Sarah are quite a couple.
Stephen	Well, I'll tell you this, Dominic. I don't know where I'd be without Sarah.
Hugh	Ah.
Stephen	Amazing woman. I think I love her more now than when I first met her. Be nothing without her. Lost. A shadow. Nothing. A blank. A zero.
Hugh	Mm.
Stephen	God I love her.
Hugh	Right. Thing is. Mm. Well. You know Mary and I have been going through a sticky patch lately?
Stephen	*(Surprised)* No. No, I didn't know that. A sticky patch.
Hugh	Yes.
Stephen	What sort of sticky patch?
Hugh	Well, just a general sort of, you know, sticky patch really.
Stephen	Oh dear. Nasty things sticky patches.
Hugh	They can be, certainly. You and Sarah have never . . . ?
Stephen	What? No. Not us. We're a team. Never had a sticky patch between us. Do you know in the fifteen years we've been married, I've never so much as looked at another woman.
Hugh	Really?
Stephen	Well, except my mother of course.
Hugh	Um . . .
Stephen	But then you have to look at your own mother,

don't you? Rude not to. And I know Sarah's
the same.

Hugh   She's never . . . ?

Stephen   No. She'd never betray me.

Hugh   She'd never, for instance, have a ten year love
affair with, say, your best friend, for the sake of,
say, argument, say?

Stephen   Sarah? No. She'd rather cut the legs off her
favourite table. Faithful as the day is long.

Hugh   Right.

Stephen   Anyway. This frank talk.

Hugh   Ah.

Stephen   You had something you wanted to say?

Hugh   Right. Yes.

Stephen   Fire away then.

Hugh   This isn't easy. It's just that – well, that ten year-
old love affair I mentioned –

Stephen   Mary.

Hugh   What?

Stephen   Oh no. Don't tell me. You've discovered that your
wife Mary has been having an affair. Dominic, I
don't know what to say.

Hugh   No, no. Mary wouldn't betray me, I know that –
that's what makes it all so difficult.

Stephen   I was going to say. I was pretty sure Mary and I
have kept it pretty discreet.

Hugh   It's the other way round, I – what?

Stephen   What?

Hugh   What did you say just now?

158

Stephen   Oh nothing. Just that I was sure Mary and I had been far too discreet for you to notice that we've been having a wild affair under your very nose for the last – twelve years I should say. At the very least.

Hugh   You and Mary have been . . .

Stephen   Oh God yes.

Hugh   But you said you would never look at another woman apart from Sarah and your mother.

Stephen   And Mary, obviously. That goes without saying.

Hugh   Well, that makes what I was going to say a lot easier then.

Stephen   Oh yes?

Hugh   It may interest you to know that your beloved Sarah and I have also been having an affair for . . . well for eleven years anyway.

Stephen   I beg your pardon? You and Sarah?

Hugh   Yes, I thought that might shake you up a bit.

Stephen   You pair of deceitful, two-timing –

Enter Sarah and Mary.

Mary   Hello, you two.

Sarah   Look at them both, up with the whisky bottle. I don't know.

Hugh   Sarah. Darling, is it true that you and, that the pair of you have been . . .

Stephen   Mary, tell me. It isn't true that the two of you have . . . is it? Tell me it isn't.

Sarah and Mary look at each other and sigh.

Sarah	We were going to tell you anyway, weren't we darling?
Mary	Yes, we were. Tonight in fact.
Sarah	Mary and I have been having an affair for the last fourteen years.
Mary	A very passionate affair.
Sarah	Strikingly passionate.
Hugh	You what?
Mary	I don't know how you found out.
Sarah	*(To Mary)* You didn't leave the thingy lying around did you?
Stephen	No, I meant you and Dominic. You and Dominic have been having an affair for the last eleven years at least.
Hugh	And you and Matthew, Mary.
Sarah	Oh that. Well that was just a diversion really.
Stephen	Oh was it? Well, Matthew, it makes it a lot easier for us to tell them, doesn't it?
Hugh	It certainly does. It may interest you to know that Dominic and I have been – how shall I phrase it?
Stephen	Bed-mates?
Sarah	Lovers?
Mary	Sex-friends?
Stephen	Joy-partners?
Sarah	Bliss buddies?
Hugh	Yes, well, any one of those for the past – what?
Stephen	Hoo, it's got to be at least eighteen or twenty hasn't it?
Hugh	Yes, for the last eighteen or twenty years.

160

Sarah	Well.
Mary	Frankly.
Sarah	So. You're saying that we have all been to bed with each other.
Stephen	That seems to be about the size of it, yes.
Mary	Though separately.
Hugh	Yes, separately, obviously.
Stephen	In every possible combination.
Sarah	Well. What a kerfuffle. What a business.
Mary	I don't know what to say.
Stephen	It is something of a how-do-you-do, isn't it?
Hugh	Well. So. What do we do?
Stephen	I should have thought it was obvious.
Mary	You mean . . . ?
Sarah	Only thing to do.
Hugh	What?
Sarah	Let's all go to bed.
Hugh	Oh. Right.

They all trot off to bed.

VOX
POP

Stephen *(Smelling a bottle of something and handing it back)* I don't know. Kenneth Baker perhaps. Nicholas Wychell?

Café

Stephen enters a café. Hugh is behind the counter,
wearing an apron and wiping the counter.

Stephen   Morning.

Hugh   Morning.

Stephen   I'd like a tuna sandwich and a tea, please.

Hugh   So would I, to be perfectly honest.

Stephen   I beg your pardon?

Hugh   Well I don't know about the tuna sandwich –
maybe a doughnut – but I'd certainly like a tea.
I'm dying of thirst.

Stephen   Oh dear, well, can I have one as well?

Hugh   What?

Stephen   A tea.

Hugh   You're asking me?

Stephen   Yes.

Hugh   Oh, ahaha. I think there's been a bit of a
misunderstanding. I don't actually work here.

Stephen   Don't you?

Hugh   No.

Stephen   Oh I'm so sorry. I thought . . .

Hugh   Oh, the apron and everything . . . yes. No I don't
work here. No no no. Haha. That's quite funny
actually.

They both look down the counter, as if to find
the owner.

162

Stephen Well . . . is it closed?

Hugh I don't think so. They'd have put the sign up.

Stephen Yes, I thought it said 'open'.

Hugh Yeah, I think it's open. Cor, I could murder a doughnut, couldn't you?

Stephen Actually yes, a doughnut would be nice.

Hugh I was thinking maybe I could just take one, and then leave the money on the side. What d'you reckon?

Stephen It's a possibility, I suppose.

Hugh 'Course, I don't know how much they are.

Stephen Errm . . .

Hugh Yes?

Stephen Well, if you don't work here, why are you behind the counter?

Hugh Me?

Stephen Yes.

Hugh I'm an undercover policeman.

Stephen Are you?

Hugh Yeah.

Stephen I see.

Hugh Phwor. Those doughnuts are driving me potty. I'm going to have to put them away in a minute.

Stephen Right, yes. You're not very far undercover, are you?

Hugh How d'you mean?

Stephen Well, I mean what's the point of being undercover, if you're going to tell me that you're undercover?

Hugh *(Quite a long pause)* Actually, that's quite a good point.

163

Stephen	Yes.
Hugh	What you're saying is, I shouldn't have told you that I was an undercover policeman?
Stephen	Precisely.
Hugh	Yeah, that's a good point. Because basically, you now know that I'm a policeman.
Stephen	Yes.
Hugh	So the whole reason for me putting on this apron and standing here since eight o'clock this morning . . . is, well, wasted really.
Stephen	I'd have thought so. I mean, it's none of my business.
Hugh	No no no. Don't ever say that. Don't ever say it's none of your business. No, we need the public to come forward. Believe me, we're very grateful.
Stephen	Not at all.
Hugh	Of course, we also need the public to shut up and not tell anyone else that I'm a policeman.
Stephen	Well of course.
Hugh	Good. That is a very good point, though. Don't say you're an undercover policeman. Yeah. Thanks.
Stephen	So, are you waiting for some criminal or something?
Hugh	That's right, funnily enough, yes. I'm waiting for a criminal, and when he enters the premises, let me put it this way, he can expect a warm reception.
Stephen	I see. That should be exciting.
Hugh	People often say that, but no, it's not exciting. It's ninety-nine per cent routine legwork.
Stephen	Right.

164

Hugh	You're not a criminal by any chance, are you?
Stephen	Me?
Hugh	Yes.
Stephen	No.
Hugh	Oh good. Because I'd have had to give you a warm reception if you were.
Stephen	But then of course, I probably wouldn't tell you if I was.
Hugh	Yeah. Right.
Stephen	Now that I know you're a policeman.
Hugh	Oh I get you. You wouldn't tell me, because you now know I'm a policeman.
Stephen	Yes. That's if I was the criminal.
Hugh	Right. Right. Are you the criminal?
Stephen	No.
Hugh	Oh good.
Stephen	But the point is, I might be.
Hugh	Oh hold up, you've gone all strange again. You just said you weren't.
Stephen	I'm not.
Hugh	Good.
Stephen	But I might be.
Hugh	This is getting stupid.
Stephen	Not really. You see, if I was a criminal, I wouldn't tell you that I was. If I wasn't, I also wouldn't tell you that I was. So just because I say I'm not, doesn't mean I'm not. A criminal.
Hugh	Slippery sod, aren't you?

Stephen	I beg your pardon?
Hugh	You read a lot of books, I suppose?
Stephen	Well, you know . . .
Hugh	One of my regrets about the police force. No time for reading.
Stephen	Mmm. Pity.
Hugh	Do you want to share a doughnut with me?
Stephen	Er, no thanks.

Hugh breaks a doughnut in two, and gives one half to Stephen.

Hugh	There you go.
Stephen	No, really I won't thank you.
Hugh	There you go.
Stephen	No.
Hugh	Take it.
Stephen	No!

Hugh pushes half the doughnut into Stephen's face.

What are you doing?

Hugh	Giving you half this doughnut.
Stephen	I don't want it!
Hugh	You think I'm stupid.
Stephen	What?
Hugh	Just because you've read books and I haven't, you think I'm stupid.
Stephen	No I don't.
Hugh	If you didn't want a doughnut, you'd say you

wanted a doughnut. So just because you're a criminal doesn't mean that I don't have to give you a doughnut, because you've said you didn't want a doughnut in the first place which is actually what you'd say if this doughnut was a policeman.

Stephen   You're mad.

Hugh   Mad am I? Your first mistake. I never told you I was mad. I told you I was a policeman. But you've just said that I'm a mad policeman. How could you have known that, without me telling you? So I must have told you. Except that I didn't, so how do you know?

Stephen   It's obvious.

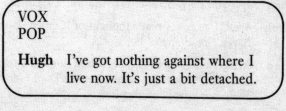

VOX
POP

Hugh   I've got nothing against where I live now. It's just a bit detached.

Judge Not

Hugh is a judge in a full-bottomed wig. Stephen is counsel with a full bottom. He is cross-examining a female witness, Deborah.

Stephen So, Miss Talliot, you expect the court to believe that on the evening of the fourteenth of November last year, the very year, I would remind the court, on which the crime that my client is accused of committing took place, you just happened to be walking in the park?

Deborah That is correct.

Stephen That is what?

Deborah Correct.

Stephen Oh it's correct, is it? I see. Am I right in understanding, Miss Talliot, that the American writer Gertrude Stein was a self-confessed Lesbian?

Deborah I believe so.

Stephen You believe so? Gertrude Stein remains one of the most celebrated American female novelists of the century, Miss Talliot. Her lesbotic tendencies are a matter of public record.

Deborah Yes.

Stephen But you only 'believe' that she was a Lesbian?

Deborah Well, I've never really thought of it much. I haven't read any of her works.

Stephen Miss Talliot, there is a bookshop not two streets away from your 'flat' where the works of Gertrude Stein are openly on display.

Deborah   Oh.

Stephen   Yes; 'oh'. And yet you would have us believe that
somehow, on the many occasions on which you
must, in the course of your duties as a woman,
have passed this shop while shopping, failed
entirely to enter and buy any book published by
this openly Sapphic authoress?

Hugh   Mr Foley, I'm afraid I really fail to see where this
line of questioning is leading us.

Stephen   With your permission m'lud, I am trying to
establish that this witness has been guilty of
weaving a tissue of litanies, that far from being the
respectable president of a children's charity and
ambassador's daughter that my learned friend the
counsel for the prosecution would have us believe,
she is in fact an active, promiscuous and voracious
Lesbite.

Hugh   I see. Carry on. But I must warn you, Mr Foley,
that if you attempt to ballyrag or bulldoze the
witness I shall take a very dim view of it.

Stephen   Your lordship is most pretty.

Hugh   Very well then, you may proceed.

Stephen   Are you aware Miss Talliot –

Deborah   It's Mrs in fact.

Stephen   Oh. Oh, I do beg your pardon. If you wish to
make so much of it, then I will certainly not
stand in your way, 'Mrs' Talliot, if that is how you
prefer to be known.

Deborah   It is how my husband prefers me to be known.

Stephen   Your husband the well-known Bishop?

Deborah   Yes.

Stephen   A bishop in a religion, the Church of – ah –

	England, I believe it calls itself, which owns land on which houses have been built, houses in which it is statistically probable that private acts of Lesbian love have been committed?
Hugh	Mr Foley, I fear I must interrupt you again. I myself am a member of this same church. Are we to imply from the tenor of your thrust that I am a Lesbian?
Stephen	Your lordship misunderstands me.
Hugh	I hope so. I hope the day is far distant on which I could be accused of making love to a woman! Ha, ha, ha.
Stephen	Certainly, m'love. I never meant to imply . . .
Hugh	Attraction to women, however, repellent as it may be to persons of sensibility, is not in itself a crime.
Stephen	I love your lordship.
Hugh	We must therefore remember, Mr Foley, in our enthusiasm to get to this bottom, that Mrs Talliot is not on trial, she is a witness. However depraved and wicked her acts of lust, they – in all their degenerate and disgusting perversion – are not the subject of this assize, bestial as they may be.
Stephen	I am yours for ever, m'dear.
Hugh	Please continue.
Stephen	I do not wish, 'Mrs Talliot' to submit the court to any more details of your sordid and disreputable erotic career than is necessary. I merely wish to enquire how it might be that you expect a jury to believe the testimony of a monstrous bull-dyke of your stamp against the word of a respectable businessman?
Deborah	I am merely reporting what I saw.
Stephen	What you saw? What you saw through eyes

170

dimmed with lust? What you saw maddened by
the noxious juices of your notorious practices?

Deborah   What I saw on my way back from the parish
council meeting.

Stephen   Is it not a fact that the words 'parish council' are
an anagram of 'lispian crouch'?

Deborah   Er . . .

Stephen   You hesitate, Miss Toilet!

Deborah   I was . . .

Stephen   You stand condemned out of your own soiled and
contaminated mouth.

Deborah   I –

Stephen   No further questions.

Deborah   Well . . .

Hugh   You may stand down, Miss Lesbian.

Deborah   Oh. And will you be in for tea tonight, Jeremy?

Stephen   Certainly, mother. *(Louder)* Call Sir Anthony
Known-Bender.

VOX
POP

Stephen   Of course crime is bound to
be on the increase. If you're
the kind of person who wants
to start a satellite broadcasting
channel, but you can't get a
licence, crime is the obvious
alternative.

Psychiatrist

Hugh, American, is standing, Stephen, English, lies on a couch.

Hugh   Are you at ease and relaxed, Mr Lloyd?

Stephen   Yes, very. This is a very comfortable chair.

Hugh   That is no accident, Mr Lloyd. It was designed by a friend of mine, to my specifications, purposely to relax you and place you fully at your ease.

Stephen   Well it is very comfortable.

Hugh   My friend will be delighted to hear that. Now, Frank – I shall be calling you Frank through the duration of these sessions. Okay by you?

Stephen   Fine.

Hugh   I have found that that also helps relax you into a state where you feel able to talk freely with me. Is it working?

Stephen   Yes.

Hugh   Good. Now . . .

Stephen   My name is Jonathan, I don't know if that –

Hugh   Good. Already we're finding out new things. Now Frank, I want you to take a deep breath through your mouth.

Stephen   *(Doing so)* Haah!

Hugh   Fine. Now I'd like you to breathe out through your nose.

Stephen snots slightly in obeying this request.

In through the mouth, out through the nose. Do you know what this is called, Frank?

172

Stephen   Breathing.

Hugh   That's nice. Frank, this is called inter-oral, extra-nasal respiratory relaxant therapy, and – as the name implies – this is an American technique. Good and calm and regular. Frank, I want now that you should allow your mind to take you backward in time. Think yourself back and back and back.

Stephen   Right.

Hugh   Have you gone back?

Stephen   Yes.

Hugh   You've gone back. What do you see in your mind's eye, Frank?

Stephen   The Spanish Armada.

Hugh   Frank, you may have gone back too far there. I'm talking of your memories Frank. Your childhood status. I want to investigate all the sense data of your infancy. Go back to when you were in second grade.

Stephen   What?

Hugh   Second grade.

Stephen   I don't know what that is. I've never understood it when people talk about grades and semesters in films.

Hugh   OK Frank, maintain your respiratory rhythms and let's turn then, if we may, to your dreams. You dream, Frank?

Stephen   Yes I do, yes as it happens, yes.

Hugh   You do? Well that's fine. Are you able at this time to recall to the surface of your consciousness any recurrent nocturnal dream sequences for me?

Stephen   Well I do have one recurring dream as a matter of fact.

Hugh	Well now, let's take time off Frank, to analyse that sequence together.
Stephen	It is rather a strange dream.
Hugh	Is it Frank, a dream of an erotic nature I wonder?
Stephen	No, not really.
Hugh	Oh. Well I'd still like to hear it.
Stephen	As I say it's a bit odd.
Hugh	Ordinarily, Frank, the more bizarre or outré the dream, the more readily susceptible to positive interpretation it thusly renders itself to become. On the converse side of the bull-pen, simpler dream experiences are more resistant to explication and offer a much more complex morphology to the professional inquirer bold enough howso to venture therein.
Stephen	I see.
Hugh	But hey, Frank! That's my problem. You've got a dream, let's share it. What do you say?
Stephen	Are you sure this is going to get us anywhere?
Hugh	Depends where you want to be, Frank.
Stephen	Well . . .
Hugh	Where do you want to be?
Stephen	Well I want –
Hugh	I want to be there too, Frank. I want to take you there. *(Putting his arm on Stephen's shoulder)* Don't be scared. Do I scare you, Frank?
Stephen	No, not really.
Hugh	You sure about that?
Stephen	Well, a bit perhaps.
Hugh	*(Incredibly loudly)* I'm going to kill you!

Stephen *(Starting)* Jesus!

Hugh That scared you, didn't it?

Stephen Yes. Yes it did, actually.

Hugh Good, I like to know the thresholds within which I have to operate. Putting my hand on your shoulder did not scare you. Shouting loudly in your ear that I was going to kill you, did. Those are my limits. My ceiling and floor if you will.

Stephen Do you want to hear this dream or not?

Hugh I very much want to hear this dream, Frank. I do really. Shoot.

Stephen Well, I'm in a corridor –

Hugh Frank, I have a small tape-recorder here. Do you mind if I – ?

Stephen No, no. Good idea. This is quite a complicated dream.

Hugh Thank you.

Stephen I'm in a big building. I think it's a hospital . . .

Hugh switches on his tape-recorder: pop music comes out. Hugh taps his feet and joins in the singing.

What are you . . . ?

Hugh Please continue, Frank.

Stephen I think it's a hospital, but it isn't. It's some kind of institution. There's a big staircase, a uniformed man at the top. Janitor or something. He beckons to me . . . look, I can't concentrate with this going on.

Hugh *(Turning it off)* I do most sincerely beg your pardon, Frank. Please continue.

Stephen Well, anyway, the janitor beckons to me and then I wake up.

Hugh   You wake up. I see. Now this sounds . . .

Stephen   And almost immediately I'm chosen for a
              bathroom wall.

Hugh   Frank, I've never thought of myself as a stupid
              man, but even so I think I'm going to need a little
              help understanding that last sentence. You were
              chosen for a bathroom wall.

Stephen   Well the thing is, you see, I haven't woken up at
              all. I've only woken up in the dream. I wake up
              and find that I'm the colour blue.

Hugh   The colour blue.

Stephen   That's right. And somebody chooses me for their
              bathroom wall.

Hugh   I see. And do you then become the colour of
              that wall?

Stephen   No. As it happens, I'm a particular shade of
              blue that's very difficult to get in the shops. The
              bathroom wall ends up with a bit too much green
              in it. But we get on reasonably well.

Hugh   I'm sorry?

Stephen   The colour of the bathroom wall and I get on
              pretty well. There are no hard feelings.

Hugh   I see. This bathroom, Frank. Does it belong
              to a lady?

Stephen   Er . . . yes, I think so.

Hugh   And she likes to bathe in this bath in this
              bathroom?

Stephen   Well I suppose so.

Hugh   Are you attracted to her?

Stephen   Well no. I'm the colour blue, how could I . . . ?

Hugh   But she's attracted to you.

Stephen   Well . . .

Hugh   She chose you, Frank. Out of all the other colours, she chose you.

Stephen   Yes.

Hugh   There you go. She was attracted to you, Frank.

Stephen   She chose me because I reminded her of the colour of a bruise she once had on her inner thigh.

Hugh   Now we're getting somewhere, Frank. You remember being the colour of this bruise?

Stephen   Vaguely.

Hugh   This is an interesting sequence, Frank. What happens next?

Stephen   I tell you how my dream continues, I think.

Hugh   Right.

Stephen   I find myself in the corridor in a large house just outside Taunton and Prince Edward is running towards me, he's about to bowl a cricket ball at me and I haven't got a bat. Prince Edward is running in to bowl and I haven't got a bat. What does that mean?

Hugh   Just may be a little early to say yet, Frank.

Stephen   But suddenly I find it isn't Prince Edward after all, it's Bob Holness.

Hugh   Come again for me?

Stephen   Bob Holness. You know, *'Blockbusters'*. Bob turns to me and I catch sight of his face, it's a twisted grinning mask of contorted hatred and frenzy. I look down and I find I have got a bat. I didn't have a bat when it was Prince Edward but I did when it was Bob Holness. Why? Why? Am I mad?

177

Hugh Mad? Frank, 'mad' is not a word I like to use.
Let's just say that half of us is always 'mad',
disordered, wild and the other half is sane,
rational, in control.

Stephen Oh I see. You mean there's two sides to every
person?

Hugh No, I mean the two of us. Half of us is sane,
that's me, and the other half is mad, that's
you, Frank.

Stephen I must say you seem rather unorthodox. The last
man I saw just gave me a couple of fillings.

Hugh Dentistry has made many advances, Frank.

Stephen Obviously.

VOX
POP

Hugh Yeah, I've been there once
or twice, but I didn't much
like it. There's another one
on the A12 which I think
is better.

Madness

*Stephen addresses the camera, the way he often does.
He is talking to Dr Marjorie who is a distinguished-
looking woman, wearing a badge that says 'Say no to
madness'.*

Stephen Every day in Britain, more than ten million
people are mad. That's the worrying conclusion
contained in a report just published entitled 'Is
Britain Turning Into a Nation Of Mad People?'
Dr Mijory Marjorie is with me now. Dr Marjorie,
just how serious is this problem . . .

Deborah It's very serious in . . .

Stephen Wait a minute, I haven't finished.

Deborah Sorry.

Stephen . . . in real terms?

Deborah *(Pause)* OK?

Stephen Yes, go on.

Deborah It's very serious indeed. In 1957, when records
began, we were, I think, the sixth maddest country
in Europe. Whereas last year's figures show
that now, Britain, I'm afraid, leads the European
Community . . .

Stephen And it is a community, isn't it?

Deborah Yes . . . Britain now leads Europe in terms of
being mad.

Stephen That's a worrying trend, certainly.

Deborah You're very kind.

Stephen Not at all. Now, Dr Marjorie, in case any viewers have just this moment tuned in, would you mind having this whole conversation all over again?

Deborah Fine with me.

Stephen Is Britain turning into a nation of mad people? Dr Mijory Marjorie is with me now. Dr Marjorie, how serious is this problem, in real terms?

Deborah Not particularly.

Stephen Not particularly what?

Deborah Serious.

Stephen Isn't it?

Deborah No.

Stephen I see. Right. When we talk about Britain being one of the maddest countries in Europe, exactly what sort of madness are we talking about?

Deborah All sorts really – from the kind of madness that leads people to put on a hat whenever they get into a car, to the really extreme madness shown by the sort of people who write to 'Points of View'.

Stephen Interesting. That's quite a broad basket of madness isn't it?

Deborah I think we've been pretty thorough.

Stephen Right. Now, for those viewers who have only just tuned in right this second, I think it might be worth you investing in a copy of the *Radio Times*, don't you? So that you can plan your viewing properly. After all, you wouldn't start reading a book at chapter five, would you?

Deborah You would if the first four chapters were rubbish.

Stephen Oh be quiet. Now turning to the causes behind or beneath or even slightly to one side of Britain's increasing madness . . . in a sense, what are they?

Deborah Well, we examined a number of factors . . .

Stephen Sorry, who is 'we'?

Deborah My mother and I.

Stephen Fine.

Deborah . . . and a woman called Alice.

Stephen Good.

Deborah And we came up with some very interesting results. Essentially, madness is like charity. It begins in the home.

Stephen Christ that's interesting.

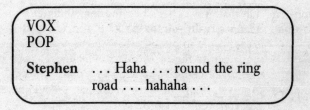

VOX
POP

Stephen . . . Haha . . . round the ring road . . . hahaha . . .

Fascism

*Hugh and Stephen are in white tie, drinking brandy,
perhaps in a clubby sort of place. Maybe a portrait of
Hitler above a mantelpiece.*

Hugh   Gayle?

Stephen   Yes, Leonard?

Hugh   How are we going to do it, I wonder?

Stephen   Do what?

Hugh   How are we going to make Fascism popular in this
country? Popular and exciting.

Stephen   Oh that. Yes. That's become something of a
madness with you, hasn't it?

Hugh   I believe it has become something of a madness
with me.

Stephen   And yet, if anyone were to ask me, I would never
say you were a mad person.

Hugh   I believe I pay you well enough for that service?

Stephen   Indeed yes. I didn't mean . . .

Hugh   Perhaps it's that little touch of madness that keeps
us all sane.

Stephen   Yes. I doubt it.

Hugh   But how are we to do it? How are we to make
Fascism exciting and important?

Stephen   We must reach out to the young people.

Hugh   You think?

Stephen   Certainly. After all, the young people are the

seedcornerstone of our society. The young people
are the future.

Hugh   Yes. Or at least they will be.

Stephen   No. They are.

Hugh   Are they?

Stephen   Yes. They will be the present, but they are
the future.

Hugh   Well well. So how can we make fascism live
among the young people?

Stephen   We could advertise.

Hugh   Gayle, my dear old mucker, what are you thinking
of? Advertise?

Stephen   I am thinking, Leonard, that we must use today's
tools for today's job.

Hugh   Go on.

Stephen   If we are to be successful.

Hugh   Yes.

Stephen   In our venture.

Hugh   Yes?

Stephen   That's it, I'm afraid.

Hugh   I see. And what are today's tools, in your opinion?

Stephen   Oh there are so many tools around today. Look
at advertising. Pop music. Films. Magazines.
Everywhere images of sexuality and coolness.

Hugh   Coolness.

Stephen   Coolness. Hipness. Laid backness. Not being a
pratness.

Hugh   And so we must make fascism . . .

Stephen   Cool.

Hugh	Cool.
Stephen	First, we must invent a fashion in clothing.
Hugh	Mmm. There must be leather.
Stephen	Leather, yes.
Hugh	And lace.
Stephen	Leather and lace, yes.
Hugh	With cotton facings.
Stephen	Excellent. Already you see, we have a look.
Hugh	And where shall we find them, these young people?
Stephen	Wherever blood and money and sexy talk flow freely, there will you find the young.
Hugh	And what will we say? How will we persuade them to surrender their ice-skating and their jazz music and turn to Fascism?
Stephen	Mm. Leonard, I wonder if you're not a little out of touch.
Hugh	Gayle, please. You are my lieutenant. My side-plate.
Stephen	Indeed.
Hugh	Tell me what I must say.
Stephen	You must say to the young people – Oh young people. You who are young and thrusting and urgent, there is a beat, a sound, a look that's new, that's you, that's positively yes!
Hugh	They'll laugh at me.
Stephen	At first . . . and ultimately, yes. But in the middle, they'll listen.
Hugh	Hmm. Alright. Boys and girls, dig what I am about

to say. Fascism is cool. Fascism is leather and lace with cotton facings.

Stephen   Good.

Hugh   Throw away those transistor radios. Come on out from those steamy parlours where the coffee is cheap and the love is free. Join us in our movement.

Stephen   And while their bodies jerk and jig to the music of those words, we must somehow introduce the subject of segregating races and abolishing elections.

Hugh   We could give away sachets of face-cream in our magazines.

Stephen   And for the women?

Hugh   Gayle. There is no place for women in our thousand year order.

Stephen   But Leonard, women do have certain useful functions.

Hugh   Such as?

Stephen   News reading.

Hugh   Why do you always insist on calling it that?

Stephen   It excites me.

Hugh   Now on the subject of racial purity, perhaps a national advertising campaign?

Stephen   Excellent.

Hugh   I will present it.

Stephen   Oh but you can't.

Hugh   And why not pray?

Stephen   Because God doesn't exist.

Hugh   No, I mean – and why not ... *(Pause)* pray?

Stephen	Because God does not ... *(Pause)* exist.
Hugh	Never mind. Why can't I front this national advertising campaign?
Stephen	Because your grandmother was a quarter Italian. I shall present the commercials.
Hugh	You? You, whose godfather is Jewish?
Stephen	At least my sister didn't marry a Welshman.
Hugh	Better marry a Welshman than eat Greek yoghurt.
Stephen	Rather Greek yoghurt than Cornish ice-cream.
Hugh	Stop, stop! Don't you see? They are turning us against each other. We shall present the commercials together.
Stephen	Yes. Together.
Hugh	Our slogan shall be – 'Good old Fascism. As true today as it's always been.'
Stephen	But Leonard, my dear old acquaintance, surely this is a new Fascism?
Hugh	Alright. 'New Ph balanced Fascism, a whole new world of natural goodness, right there in the cup.'
Stephen	Cup?
Hugh	Why not?
Stephen	What about – 'Maureen Lipman, with some letters from you about new Fascism'.
Hugh	Would she do it?
Stephen	I don't see why not.
Hugh	I have it. 'If you thought Fascism was just goose-steps and funny hats, then take a look at what we've been doing. Available in matchpots too.'
Stephen	*Das Sieg wird unser sein,* as they say in Germany.

186

Hugh   Do you hate anyone enough to give them your last pot-noodle?

Stephen   Fascism. Half the fat, all the taste. That's the Fascist promise.

Hugh   From Lenor.

Stephen   It's Ideal.

Hugh   I wish I was young.

Stephen   Me too.

> **VOX POP**
>
> **Hugh**   It's just well laid out, you see. If you can imagine that the four star pumps are lined up there, and they've got the diesel and two star pumps opposite ... well you see I much prefer that.

Jeremiah Beadle

Hugh is a bank teller. Stephen approaches the counter wearing some sort of mask and carrying a sawn-off shotgun.

Stephen Be clever.

Hugh I beg your pardon?

Stephen Be clever. If you even breathe too loud, I'll blow you in half. Now, slowly and carefully, open the till and take out all the notes.

Hugh All the notes?

Stephen All the notes.

Hugh Yes. Is your account actually with this branch?

Stephen What?

Hugh If not, I'll have to make a phone call. Shouldn't take long.

Stephen If you even look at a telephone, I'll spread your brains all over the wall. I'm robbing the bank.

Hugh Robbing the . . . oh God.

Stephen Now just take it easy.

Hugh Oh God.

Stephen Mouth shut. Nice and relaxed. Put all the notes into this bag.

Hugh Don't kill me.

Stephen Just do it, alright?

Hugh Yes, yes. All the notes . . .

Stephen That's it. Nice and easy.

Hugh nervously takes out all the cash, then suddenly stops.

Hugh   Oh oh. Wait a minute.

Stephen   What?

Hugh   Oh I don't believe it. I don't believe it.

Stephen   Come on, I haven't got all day.

Hugh   Who put you up to this?

Stephen   Put me up . . . ?

Hugh   It was Carol, wasn't it? I knew it! She's crazy. Tscch! Where's the camera then?

Stephen   What are you talking about?

Hugh   You're that Jeremy Beadle, aren't you?

Stephen   What!?

Hugh   I didn't recognise you at first. I'll kill her! She's a right minx. Oh I feel such an idiot!

Stephen   Listen, you twerp, put all the money . . .

Hugh   I must say this is brilliant. You people are so clever. So when's it going to be on the television?

Stephen   Look, I am not Jeremy bleeding Beadle! Now put the notes in the bag.

Hugh   'Course you'll have to bleep that out, won't you?

Stephen   What?

Hugh   Jeremy bleeding Beadle. You can't really say Jeremy bleeding Beadle on family television. Unless of course 'Bleeding' is actually your middle name.

Stephen   Look, I am not Jeremy Beadle. I don't look anything like Jeremy Beadle.

Hugh   Well not with that mask on, obviously.

Stephen removes the mask.

Stephen Satisfied?

Hugh That's brilliant.

Stephen What is?

Hugh You've got a false head on, have you? That's incredible.

Stephen If you don't fill that bag and pass it over in ten seconds, I'll kill you.

Hugh I can't wait to see this.

Stephen One, two . . .

Hugh Actually, to tell the truth, I used to prefer 'Candid Camera' . . .

Stephen Five, six . . .

Hugh You just stole their idea, really, didn't you?

Stephen Nine . . .

Hugh Oh I just wish I'd put that other shirt on this morning. Still . . .

Stephen fires into Hugh's chest. Lots of blood.

(Dying) You will send me a tape, won't you?

VOX
POP

Hugh And if you don't like the shape you can scoop it out with your finger.

Architect

*Stephen is sitting behind, yes, a desk. On the desk
there is what appears to be an architect's model of
a fairly pleasing housing estate. Nicely done, trees, a
stream, model people walking dogs and so on. Hugh is
explaining it.*

Hugh   And basically I think ... or what I hope I've
managed to achieve with this design is a new
direction. The emphasis is very much on the
quality of people's day to day lives. I know it
doesn't correspond exactly to the initial brief, but
I hope you'll agree it has qualities that really set
it apart from any other contemporary design. Ha.
That's it really. I'm very excited by it.

Stephen   Yes.

Hugh   So what do you think?

Stephen   Ahem. Mr Braganza ...

Hugh   Please be honest.

Stephen   I will. I will. But first of all can I ask you why you
chose to depart from the ... er ... shall we say
traditional ... ?

Hugh   You mean the old shoe box approach.

Stephen   That's it.

Hugh   The strict, rectangular lines ...

Stephen   That's right. Shoe box.

Hugh   Well to be honest, Mr Catchpole, that style is out,
it's dead. Brutalism, modernism, post-modernism,
all those isms are finished with. We've got to look
at people's lives.

Stephen   Yes, quite. The thing is, when we asked for a shoe box, we did actually mean a box for putting shoes in. We are a shoe manufacturer, you see. And we really do need to put our shoes in a box.

Hugh   Oh I know that. I know that. But by carrying on with the same old rectangular prisons, you're only stifling the human spirit. I'm trying to free the human spirit.

Stephen   Well that's ... that's fine. But you see, I'm left with the problem of where to put our shoes. I need a box to put our shoes in, you see? I need a shoe box.

Hugh   Need? Who are we to say what's needed, in the sense of some fancy design idea that's going to blight the lives of generations to come?

Stephen   I don't think our shoe boxes have blighted any generations.

Hugh   Well I wouldn't be too sure about that.

Stephen   Nick. Let me put it this way. To me, a shoe box is just a machine for keeping shoes in.

Hugh   Oh yes? And to hell with the human spirit, that's what you're saying.

Stephen   Not really.

Hugh   I know what it is. It's the cost, isn't it? You're frightened of how much it's going to cost.

Stephen   No, I'm frightened of where I'm going to put our shoes.

Hugh   Well forget money. Because there are some things that can't be calculated to the last penny. I'm talking about human lives.

Stephen   Yes, you see, I'm talking about shoes.

Hugh   Oh shoes, shoes. Is that all you think about?

Stephen   When I'm at work, yes.

Hugh   Well then I feel sorry for you. In fact, I pity you.

Stephen   Well . . .

Hugh   But I'll do you a shoebox, if that's what you want. I don't know how I'll live with myself, but if that's what you want, I'll do you a nice, safe, ordinary, rectangular shoe box.

Stephen   Thank you.

Hugh picks up the model.

Hugh   I'll take this away, then.

Stephen   No no. Leave it here. I think we can find a use for it.

Hugh   What?

Stephen   Some of our workers might want to live in it.

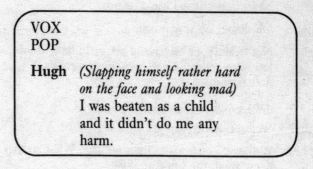

VOX
POP

Hugh   *(Slapping himself rather hard on the face and looking mad)* I was beaten as a child and it didn't do me any harm.

Critics Four

Hello, it's swivel-chair time again.

Hugh   Simon Clituris. You saw that. What do you think was happening there?

Stephen Well you see, again this was a rather trite, rather predictable – I don't know what the word is I'd use to describe it really.

Hugh   Squib?

Stephen If you like. A sort of cod spoof guying take-off pastiche parody.

Hugh   What did you make of the two central performances?

Stephen I'd have welcomed them.

Hugh   *(Laughing at this sally)* Right, right. I liked the clever and original use of words.

Stephen Oh thank you very much.

Hugh   Not at all. Your clever and original use of words has been collected into book form recently, I understand.

Stephen That's right.

Hugh   Well received?

Stephen Well, you know what critics are like. What do they know about the work we do?

Hugh   Quite so, quitely so. Quitely so-ington. But to return to that spoof cod squib guying of conventions. My main worry was that it told us nothing of the relationship between the two central characters.

Stephen   That's right. Some people may have been mildly amused by this kind of grotesquerie, but where were the truths about relationships in England today, now, this evening, this afternoon?

Hugh   You certainly couldn't see them from where I was lying.

Stephen   No, I hated it.

Hugh   That's right. Two out of ten for trying, then.

Stephen   It just wasn't your cup of tea?

Hugh   No. *(Picking up teacup)* This is my cup of tea, in fact.

Stephen   Actually, I think you'll find it's mine.

VOX POP

Hugh   The short one has got a different accent, but they both smell of Noël Edmonds to me.

Marjorie's Fall

Some sort of period sitting room. Stephen is fiddling with a clock on the mantelpiece. Hugh enters, agitated.

Hugh   Thomas! Bad news I'm afraid.

Stephen   Just a moment, John. I promised Marjorie I'd mend this clock for her. I wonder if you could give me a hand.

Hugh   Big hand?

Stephen   Little hand.

Hugh   Anyway Thomas, listen to me. I have some bad news.

Stephen   Bad news?

Hugh   It's Marjorie.

Stephen   Marjorie?

Hugh   She's had a fall.

Stephen   Marjorie's had a fall?

Hugh   I'm afraid so. She was out riding this morning on Thunderbolt, and she hadn't returned by the time Mrs Mempwaster arrived. It turns out she'd had a fall.

Stephen   Calm yourself John. Marjorie has had a fall?

Hugh   Yes.

Stephen   Off a horse?

Hugh   Well of course off a horse.

Stephen   I don't see that there's any 'of course' about it,

	John. Girls nowadays are likely to fall off anything. Doesn't have to be a horse.
Hugh	No, alright. But in this case it was.
Stephen	She could have fallen off a chair, a table, a pianoforte, anything.
Hugh	Yes, except that, in this case, she was riding a horse when it happened.
Stephen	When she fell off?
Hugh	Yes.
Stephen	So, you reasoned to yourself, Marjorie has fallen from a horse?
Hugh	That's right. Thunderbolt.
Stephen	Thunderbolt, you say?
Hugh	Yes.
Stephen	Well, Thunderbolt's a horse, alright.
Hugh	Exactly.
Stephen	Any damage?
Hugh	Too soon to say. Cavendish is examining her now.
Stephen	That old fool. What does he know about horses?
Hugh	Cavendish is examining Marjorie.
Stephen	Marjorie? Is she ill?
Hugh	No. She fell off a horse.
Stephen	Fell off a horse? Then you'd better fetch Cavendish.
Hugh	I have, Thomas. He's in the drawing room.
Stephen	Horses are very big, John.
Hugh	I know they are, Thomas.

Stephen	You fall off one of them, and anything can happen.
Hugh	Quite.
Stephen	*(Pause)* Well not 'anything'.
Hugh	No. Not 'anything'.
Stephen	I mean this clock isn't going to become Prime Minister, just because someone has fallen off a horse. I didn't mean 'anything' in that sense.
Hugh	Of course not, Thomas. Anyway Cavendish is examining her now.
Stephen	You said he was in the drawing room.
Hugh	He is. Examining Marjorie.
Stephen	And where is she?
Hugh	She's also in the drawing room.
Stephen	Hah. So they're both in the drawing room?
Hugh	Yes.
Stephen	Perhaps I was wrong. Perhaps he's not such a fool after all. How is she?
Hugh	Too soon to say. Sounds like a hell of a fall.
Stephen	From the horse?
Hugh	Yes.
Stephen	Thunderbolt?
Hugh	Yes.
Stephen	Now what the devil is Marjorie doing, falling off Thunderbolt?
Hugh	You know how Marjorie loves to ride, Thomas.
Stephen	She was riding Thomas?
Hugh	No no.
Stephen	I'm Thomas, John.

198

Hugh	I know.
Stephen	She wasn't riding me. Your story's a bit twisted there, old fellow. Doesn't add up. You said she was riding Thunderbolt.
Hugh	She was.
Stephen	She was?
Hugh	Yes.
Stephen	But she's not any longer?
Hugh	No. She fell off.
Stephen	Good God.
Hugh	I know.
Stephen	Where is she?
Hugh	In the drawing room.
Stephen	She was riding Thunderbolt in the drawing room?
Hugh	No. She fell off at Stratton Brook, where the path separates. That young fellow Cottrell found her and carried her to the drawing room.
Stephen	Stables would have been better, don't you think?
Hugh	What?
Stephen	Drawing room's no place for Thunderbolt.
Hugh	Marjorie.
Stephen	What d'you mean?
Hugh	Marjorie's in the drawing room.
Stephen	With Thunderbolt?
Hugh	No. Thunderbolt's in the stables.
Stephen	Oh. Well that's alright, then.
Hugh	It's not alright, Thomas. She's had a bad fall.

Stephen   Is she hurt?

Hugh   Too soon to say. Cavendish is with her now.

Stephen   Cavendish? He's a doctor, isn't he?

Hugh   Yes.

Stephen   I wonder if he knows anything about clocks.

> VOX
> POP
>
> **Stephen**   I started on the piano and then moved up onto the mantelpiece.

The 'Burt'

Stephen is interviewing Hugh, who is a croaky-voiced Richard Harris, stroke Peter O'Toole stroke Oliver Reed stroke my thigh sort of wildman actor.

Stephen Did you actually know Burton personally?

Hugh Oh yes. Well, in as much as anyone really 'knew' Burton. Oh yes, I was very fond of 'the Burt'. He was such a character, you see.

Stephen And of course Elizabeth Taylor . . .

Hugh Well now Liz was a joy, a dream, a treasure. If you could have seen them together . . .

Stephen Did you ever . . .

Hugh Oh yes. Many times. In fact I was best man at their wedding.

Stephen Which one?

Hugh All of them.

Stephen Now Gielgud and Richardson. You must have . . .

Hugh They never married of course.

Stephen No, but you knew them?

Hugh Oh good Lord yes. Real characters. 'The Giel' and 'the Rich' used to ask me for advice, constantly. They used to call me their 'guru'.

Stephen Now around that time, you must have met . . .

Hugh Just about everyone, really.

Stephen Good heavens.

Hugh Oh yes. I knew everyone, and everyone knew me.

201

Stephen	That's extraordinary.
Hugh	I really was very lucky.
Stephen	Mmm. What did you think of Simon Condywust?
Hugh	Simon . . .
Stephen	Condywust. Didn't you know him?
Hugh	Oh yes, I knew him. Yes, everyone knew 'the Condy'. Yes. Amazing character, he really was.
Stephen	Right. What about Margaret Limpwippydippydodo?
Hugh	Mm. Now, Margaret was fascinating. I was fascinated by her for many, many years.
Stephen	Was she an amazing character?
Hugh	No. She was a woman. The men were characters. Margaret was fascinating.
Stephen	I see. Colin FenchmoseythinkIhave?
Hugh	What a character.
Stephen	Fenella Hahahahahaspuit?
Hugh	Fascinating woman.
Stephen	Peter Weeeeeeeeeeeeeeeeeeeeeeee?
Hugh	Now there was a character. They broke the mould after they made Peter.
Stephen	Angela BrokethemouldaftertheymadePeter?
Hugh	Delightful woman.
Stephen	Cliff Richard?
Hugh	You've just made that up.

Chicken

Stephen and Deborah are having dinner in a restaurant.

Stephen   He gets all misty-eyed and he puffs himself up and says – 'I do it for my country' . . . and he stabs himself in the head with a pair of scissors. So the Irishman says . . .

Hugh enters as a waiter, pushing a trolley.

Hugh   Are you ready for your main courses now?

Stephen   Yes I think so.

Woman   Yes please.

Hugh   Excellent.

Stephen   Can I ask you something?

Hugh   Certainly.

Stephen   How do you do it?

Hugh   Do what, sir?

Stephen   How can you hear from the other side of the restaurant the exact moment I get to the punchline of a joke? You've done it four times since we arrived.

Hugh   Good question, sir. There's actually a tiny microphone hidden underneath the ashtray.

Stephen   Oh I see.

Hugh   And we have a receiver in the kitchen, so you know . . . It's very simple really.

Stephen   Right. I just wondered.

Hugh	The lamb?
Woman	Yes please.
Hugh	Very good madam.

Hugh puts a plate of lamb in front of her.

Woman	Thank you.
Stephen	Where was I? The Englishman ... er ... oh hell ...
Hugh	*(While giving her vegetables)* The Englishman said 'I do it for the Queen' and jumped out of the window ...
Stephen	That's right, yes. Then the Scotsman said 'I do it for my country' and er –
Hugh	Stabbed himself in the head with the pair of ...
Stephen	... scissors, that's right. So the Irishman said ...
Hugh	And you're having the chicken, sir?
Stephen	Tsscch. What?
Hugh	Chicken Lacroix. Prepared at your table.
Stephen	Yes, thanks very much. The Irishman ...

Hugh removes the lid of some huge graillon, to reveal a live chicken, preferably clucking.

Woman	Oh my God!
Stephen	What!?
Hugh	Chicken Lacroix.

Hugh starts to sharpen a knife.

Stephen	What are you doing?
Hugh	What am I doing?

204

Stephen	Yes.
Hugh	Sir, I have to make sure the knife is properly sharp.
Stephen	I mean this chicken . . . it's alive!
Hugh	Ha. Not for much longer, sir.
Woman	I think I'm going to be sick.
Hugh	Oh. Something wrong with the lamb, madam?
Stephen	You're not going to kill a chicken in here?
Hugh	Certainly. This, sir, is Chicken Lacroix. As you ordered. 'Fresh, plump, baby chicken, prepared at your table.'

Hugh lifts the knife.

Stephen	Wait! Don't . . . don't kill it!
Hugh	Don't kill it?
Stephen	No!
Hugh	You'd rather eat it while it's alive?
Stephen	No.
Hugh	Well then . . .
Stephen	Stop it! I'm telling you – don't kill that chicken.
Hugh	Is there a problem, sir?
Stephen	Yes there is. You cannot kill that chicken.
Hugh	Why not, sir?
Stephen	Well . . . you know.
Hugh	No.
Stephen	All the letters we'll get. It's not worth it.
Hugh	Letters?

Stephen	Yes.
Hugh	Who from?
Stephen	Oh I don't know. Mad people.
Hugh	What mad people?
Stephen	Mad people. 'Why oh why oh why oh why was my six-year-old grandmother forced to watch a chicken being hacked to death in the name of so-called entertainment?' That kind of thing.
Hugh	Well it's no worse than being hacked to death in the name of so-called lunch.
Stephen	Well I know that.
Woman	It is, actually.
Hugh	I beg your pardon?
Woman	I think it is worse.
Hugh	Oh do you?
Woman	Yes.
Hugh	Really?
Stephen	Yes well that's fair enough.
Hugh	Is it? Well let's ask the chicken, shall we? Would you rather die as part of a sketch on national television, or would you prefer just to go straight into a Tesco sandwich, unmourned and unnoticed?
Woman	That's just how I feel. I'm sorry.
Hugh	What's the matter with you? It's had a great time. We showed it the 'Blue Peter' studio, didn't we?
Stephen	Actually, I'd be happier if you didn't kill it.
Hugh	What?
Stephen	I'd be happier if you didn't kill the chicken.
Hugh	Happier? What's happiness got to do with it?

Stephen	To be honest, I never really liked the idea.
Hugh	'Never really liked'?
Woman	I'm not crazy about it either.
Hugh	Oh well obviously if everyone's just going to go squeamish at the last minute, we'll have to call it off.
Stephen	I think so.
Hugh	Right.
Stephen	On second thoughts, I'll just have a green salad.
Hugh	A green salad?
Stephen	Please.
Hugh	Very good, sir.

Hugh takes the chicken trolley and exits.

Stephen	I think that was the right decision.
Woman	So do I.
Stephen	Anyway, so the Irishman says ...

Stephen is interrupted by violent terrifying screams.

Now what are you doing?

Hugh enters with a plate of salad.

Hugh	Never heard a lettuce scream before? Frightening isn't it?
Stephen	What?
Hugh	You never knew, did you? You thought lettuces just came in little sterilised polythene bags, and grew on supermarket shelves. Never occurred to you that a lettuce might have feelings, hopes, dreams, a family ...

Stephen Bugger the lettuce! Will you let me finish my joke!?

Hugh Oh I'm sorry.

Stephen The Irishman says . . .

Cut to whatever.

> VOX
> POP
>
> **Stephen** I like the way it *starts*.

Cocoa

An old people's home. Mr Simnock's room. Bed, sofa, etc.

Stephen *(Attendant)* Alright, Mr Simnock?

Hugh *(Very, very old northerner)* Eh?

Stephen I say, are you alright, Mr Simnock?

Hugh Smimble cocoa.

Stephen Yes, you can have your cocoa in a minute. I'll draw the curtains shall I?

Hugh Eh?

Stephen I say, I'll draw the curtains – be a bit cosier. More cosy for you.

Hugh Draw the curtains, cosy that. Cocoa.

Stephen Yes, your cocoa's coming, Mr Simnock.

Hugh Curtains.

Stephen *(Drawing them)* There, that's better. Nights are drawing in now, aren't they, Mr Simnock? Getting more chilly by the day. I don't know, time just races by doesn't it? Seems like it was only yesterday that it was Christmas. Oh no, what's this? You've dropped your magazines.

Hugh Didn't like them. Rubbish they were.

Stephen I'll pick them up for you – let's see, what have we got here.

As Stephen bends down to pick up the magazines, Hugh cuffs him a mighty blow on the ear.

Ooh, there now. That wasn't very nice was it?

	Hitting me like that. What d'you want to go and do that for?
Hugh	Want me cocoa.
Stephen	Your cocoa's coming – though I'm not so sure as you deserve it, really acting up today like I shouldn't wonder. Whatever next? You're a bad man, Mr Simnock. I'll tuck you up, look.
Hugh	Ninety-two years old.
Stephen	That's right, ninety-two isn't it? Ninety-three come November.
Hugh	Ninety-two years old and I've never had oral sex.
Stephen	I should think not indeed. Oral sex! The idea.
Hugh	Never ridden a camel.
Stephen	Now you're just babbling, Mr Simnock.
Hugh	I've never watched a woman urinate.
Stephen	I shall get cross with you in a minute, I shall really.
Hugh	Never killed a man.
Stephen	Now Mr Simnock, there's a certain man that I shall start killing if he's not very careful, thank you very much.
Hugh	Never been inside an opera house. Never eaten a hamburger.
Stephen	You're a stupid silly old man and I won't have any nonsense.
Hugh	I'm fed up, me. Never done anything.
Stephen	Well, you're a bit chilly I shouldn't wonder. Your cocoa'll be along in a minute.
Hugh	Don't want any stupid cocoa.
Stephen	Now don't be contrary – you love your cocoa.

Hugh	I hate cocoa. Gets a skin on it.
Stephen	Not if you keep stirring it.
Hugh	Makes me kek that, makes me want to cat up. I want to drink milk from the breasts of a Burmese maiden.
Stephen	I don't know. What's the matter with you today, Mr Simnock? I think we'll have to put you on extra Vitamin E. Burmese maidens! In Todmorden.
Hugh	You've got bad breath you have.
Stephen	Now. Now, Mr Simnock, there's no call to be personal, I hope.
Hugh	Like rotting cabbages.
Stephen	I'm very angry with you, Mr Simnock.
Hugh	You're a great Nancy.
Stephen	I'm not a great Nancy, Mr Simnock, and you're wicked to say so.
Hugh	Great Nancy, Mary-Ann, bum-boy Nance. I bet you've never even done it.
Stephen	I won't have you talking like this Mr Simnock, I won't really.
Hugh	You shouldn't be in a place like this, your time of life.
Stephen	Someone's got to do it, Mr Simnock. Dedication, though why I bother –
Hugh	You should be out there having oral sex, killing people, watching women urinate in opera houses and eating hamburgers on camels. Drinking milk from the breasts of Nepalese maidens.
Stephen	It was Burmese last time.
Hugh	I've changed my mind. Nepalese. Instead you're

stuck here taking rude talk from an old man.
You're a Nancy, a great bog-breath Nancy.

Stephen   Ooh, you've upset me today, Mr Simnock, you
have really. I'm going out to hurry along your
cocoa and when I get back I don't want any more
nonsense. Honestly!

Exit Stephen.

Hugh   *(Calling after him)* You're a screaming Bertie
and you pong. *(To himself)* Never seen a woman
urinate, not once. Tragic waste, that.

Stephen   *(Re-entering)* Now, I managed to intercept Mrs
Gideon with the tray in the vestibule. So here's
your cocoa, and don't say you aren't a lucky man
to get it before the others.

Hugh   Hooray!

Stephen   There, that's the stuff isn't it?

Hugh   Cocoa.

Stephen   Yes. A certain naughty boy said some naughty
things though, didn't he?

Hugh   I'm sorry Brian. Right sorry.

Stephen   Well there. As soon as you see your cocoa you
mend your manners. I'm not sure I should give it
to you, now.

Hugh   Oh please, Brian.

Stephen   There you are then. That's better, isn't it?

Hugh   Lovely drop of cocoa, that.

Stephen   Berent's: that's the best.

Stephen smiles at the camera.

Advert-style voice-over

Good old Berent's cocoa. Always there. Original
or New Berent's, specially prepared for the mature
citizens in your life, with nature's added store of
powerful barbiturates and heroin.

Hugh collapses with a grin on his face.

VOX
POP

Hugh   Betty had a bit of bitter
butter and put it in her
batter and made her batter
bitter.

Naked

Stephen and Hugh are in a black limbo area. Hugh is on a monitor, Stephen is really there.

Stephen I'm afraid that we've now got to ask you to do some work, and help us a bit, ladies and gentlemen. Use you imagination, as it were.

Hugh That's right. For the purposes of this next sketch, ladies and gentlemen, we want you all to imagine that we're both naked.

Stephen Yes. I'm sorry to have to ask this of you. Speaking for ourselves, Hugh and I really wanted to go the whole way, and actually be naked for this one but, unfortunately, we ran out of money.

Hugh That's right. The budget simply wouldn't stretch that far, I'm afraid. Never mind.

Stephen Now to help you build up the picture in your minds, I should tell you that the sketch is set in a church.

Hugh That's right. Stephen will be playing a Bishop.

Stephen And Hugh will be playing the organ.

Hugh The organist.

Stephen What?

Hugh I'll be playing the organist.

Stephen The organist. Yes. But you'll be playing the organ as well?

Hugh No. No. That's the whole point. I play an organist who can't play the organ.

214

Stephen   Oh God I'm sorry. I'm sorry. Of course. Have I ruined it?

Hugh   Yes, frankly.

Stephen   I'm sorry, ladies and gentlemen.

Hugh   You'd better all stop imagining that we're naked.

Stephen   Yes stop. Hold it. It's all my fault. I'm sorry. Damn.

VOX
POP

Stephen   A man enters a bar. It was an iron bar. No, *goes into* a bar. *Walks* into a bar, that's it. A man walks into a pub, it was an iron pub. Henry Cooper used to do that one. Tommy. Tommy Bar used to walk into that one. Oh no, that can't be right.

Nipples

Stephen   Ladies and gentlemen, I think we've got to know
each other well enough over the weeks now, for
me to make a little confession. I don't want you
to be embarrassed by this. *I'm* not, and it is I
whose breast is being cleaned, not yours. The fact
is, I'm not quite as I seem. You see before you
what I have been kind enough to call a rather
lovely figure of a super and that's by and breastly
as it should be. However, and this is where I'm
going to have to ask you to be excitingly pretty,
I do have a peculiarity which I feel I must in all
softness be rather heavenly about just for a divine.
Like an increasing number of people today, I have
a pair of nipples attached to my chest, here and
to a lesser extent here, but, and this is where
I'm forced to be a little bit more delicious than
usual, while this one here, Neville, is rosy and
healthy and everything one could want, this one
Sheila is bright blue and something of a young
disappointment. Well there, in a smooth-limbed
golden-thighed way, we are. You've been patient,
you've been glossy, you've been surprisingly supple.
I've enjoyed being fabulous with you. Thank you.

Language Conversation

Stephen and Hugh are in a TV studio, talking animatedly – at least Stephen is animated.

Hugh   Well, let's talk about instead about flexibility of language – linguistic elasticity if you like.

Stephen   I think I said earlier that our language, English –

Hugh   As spoken by us –

Stephen   As we speak it, yes certainly, defines us. We are defined by our language if you will, then please, for goodness' sake, do.

Hugh   *(To camera)* Hullo! We're talking about language.

Stephen   Perhaps I can illustrate my point – let me at least try. Here's a question: is our language capable, English this is, is it capable of sustaining demagoguery?

Hugh   Demagoguery?

Stephen   Demagoguery.

Hugh   And by demagoguery you mean . . . ?

Stephen   I mean demagoguery, I mean highly-charged oratory, persuasive whipping up rhetoric. Listen to me, if Hitler had been English would we, under similar circumstances have been moved, charged up, fired by his inflammatory speeches, or should we have laughed? Er, er, er, is English too ironic a language to support Hitlerian styles, would his language simply have, have rung false in our ears?

Hugh   *(To camera)* We're talking about things ringing false in our ears.

Stephen   Alright, alright, do you mind if I compartmentalise? I hate to, but may I? May I? Is our language a function of our British cynicism, tolerance, resistance to false emotion, humour and so on, or do those qualities come *extrinsically* – *extrinsically*, from the language itself? It's a chicken and egg problem.

Hugh   *(To camera)* We're talking about chickens, we're talking about eggs.

Stephen   Let me start a leveret here: there's language, the grammar, the structure – then there's utterance. Listen to me, listen to me, there's chess and there's a game of chess. Mark the difference, mark it for me please.

Hugh   *(To camera)* We've moved on to chess.

Stephen   Imagine a piano keyboard, eighty-eight keys, only eighty-eight and yet, and yet, new tunes, melodies, harmonies are being composed upon hundreds of keyboards every day in Dorset alone. Our language, Tiger, our language, hundreds of thousands of available words, frillions of possible legitimate new ideas, so that I can say this sentence and be confident it has never been uttered before in the history of human communication: 'Hold the newsreader's nose squarely, waiter, or friendly milk will countermand my trousers.' One sentence, common words, but never before placed in that order. And yet, oh and yet, all of us spend our days saying the same things to each other, time after weary time, living by clichaic, learned response: 'I love you', 'Don't go in there', 'You have no right to say that', 'shut up', 'I'm hungry', 'that hurt', 'why should I?', 'it's not my fault', 'help', 'Marjorie is dead'. You see? That surely is a thought to take out for a cream tea on a rainy Sunday afternoon.

Hugh looks at camera, opens mouth as if to speak, decides against it. Speaks to Stephen instead.

Hugh   So to you language is more than just a means of communication?

Stephen   Er, of course it is, of course it is, of course it is. Language is a whore, a mistress, a wife, a pen-friend, a check-out girl, a complimentary moist lemon-scented cleansing square or handy freshen-up wipette. Language is the breath of God, the dew on a fresh apple, it's the soft rain of dust that falls into a shaft of morning sun when you pull from an old bookshelf a forgotten volume of erotic diaries; language is the faint scent of urine on a pair of boxer shorts, it's a half-remembered childhood birthday party, a creak on the stair, a spluttering match held to a frosted pane, the warm wet, trusting touch of a leaking nappy, the hulk of a charred Panzer, the underside of a granite boulder, the first downy growth on the upper lip of a Mediterranean girl, cobwebs long since overrun by an old Wellington boot.

Hugh   Ner-night.

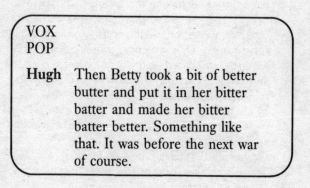

VOX
POP

Hugh   Then Betty took a bit of better butter and put it in her bitter batter and made her bitter batter better. Something like that. It was before the next war of course.

Stephen's Poem

Stephen 'Crate, a normil nighman
Hane a freethy stipe
You veen where musse is Simon
Critch botty trees a wipe.'

I first wrote the poem from which that verse was
an extract when my dear wife Enemy died. I wrote
it again in 1978 after hearing of the death of rock
music. I'd like with your kind indulgence to write
it once more. Thank you.

Stephen sits and writes.

Girlfriend's Breasts

Farmhouse kitchen set. Like a Tyne Tees TV late night religious discussion set. Stephen intrudes on Hugh who is busy reading a book. They are both foully nice.

Stephen   Who told you that you were naked?

Hugh puts the book down and looks smilingly up at Stephen.

Hugh   I'm sorry?

Stephen   I was thinking 'who told you that you were naked'?

Hugh   You may have lost me there, Arnold.

Stephen   Well, let me explain. I was thinking of that passage in the book of Genesis where Adam explains to God why he and Eve have covered themselves.

Hugh   Ah yes. If I remember that story alright, Adam says, 'we were naked and we were ashamed'.

Stephen   That's right, Glenn. And God says . . .

Hugh   'Who told you that you were naked?'

Stephen   *(As if catching sight of the camera for the first time, speaking directly into it)* We were just having a conversation, Glenn and I, about a passage in Genesis that has been intriguing me rather.

Hugh   It is fascinating isn't it? But anyway, tell me about the size of your girlfriend's breasts.

Stephen   Well, let's clear up this problem of why God should give such a complex reply to what is, on the surface, a very simple question.

Hugh   Not as simple a question, in many ways, as for instance: 'are they very big, or only quite big?'

Stephen	Well, fair point. But while not that simple, still relatively simple.
Hugh	That's right, Arnold: simpler certainly than 'is she very exciting in bed?'
Stephen	Ng. I think God was saying, 'How are you aware, Adam, of such a thing as a "state of nakedness"? How can that concept mean anything to you, unless you have eaten of the fruit whereof I said thou shouldst not eat?'
Hugh	My bet is that they are really quite substantially large. A fulsome pair of funbags, that's my bet.
Stephen	One thing at a time Glenn.
Hugh	You're right. One thing at a time. Let's take the left one first shall we? How enormous would you say that it is?
Stephen	*(Laughing)* Ha, ha! Glenn is having difficulty concentrating on our Bible Study readings because he has something of an obsession with the size of my girlfriend's breasts.
Hugh	*(Also laughing)* I like to put it this way. Arnold is having trouble concentrating on our little discussions about the size of his girlfriend's bazoncas because he is a little too interested in analysing passages from the Bible.
Stephen	We'll sort it out, don't you worry!!

They both turn to each other talking again, simultaneously.

Hugh	Say a forty-eight cup, or bigger still?
Stephen	A knowledge of good and evil, that is what the fruit contained, when Eve took it from the serpent . . . etc.

Violence

Stephen and Hugh are somewhere.

Stephen   Violence: it's a theme we've touched on before
now in this fortnightly look back on the past three
days, and I dare say it's one we'll touch on again,
and we don't apologise for that. Violence is not
something that is going to lie down and go away.

Hugh   Well put. I suppose Responsibility Television is the
phrase that best sums up our approach.

Stephen   What does Responsibility Television mean? Well
it means that we are immensely concerned that
nothing we do has a bad influence on our viewers.
Thus when I hit Hugh, like so:

Stephen hits Hugh.

We have to consider what the effect on the viewer
might be.

Hugh   Is a vulnerable, easily-led section of our audience
going to start imitating this kind of behaviour?

Stephen   Well so far in this series I have hit Hugh on no
less than a startling seven occasions. You might
think we had no thought at all as to how the young
might be influenced by this kind of senseless,
horrific violence. Would they start to imitate
it? Hugh.

Hugh   Well the interesting and inescapable conclusion
that we've come up with is yes. Because since the
series has started to be transmitted I have found,
walking along the street that I have been hit no
less than twelve times by complete strangers.

Stephen   So it looks as if the suggestible out there are actually imitating my violent behaviour patterns and striking you?

Hugh   That's right.

Stephen   Is that a worrying development?

Hugh   It's not unworrying.

Stephen   So it might be that the Milton Schulmans of this world aren't as incredibly stupid as they appear at first, second and thirty-fourth glance. We are unwittingly helping to make Britain a more violent place.

Hugh   It's beginning to look horribly like it.

Stephen   Well, let's see if we can't reverse this process. I'm going to give you a fiver now Hugh.

Stephen does so.

Would all those stupid enough to be influenced by my violent behaviour who are likely to go out onto the street and hit Hugh please watch very carefully as I now smile at Hugh, hand him another five pounds and say 'There you are old chap, there's a fiver for you. Have a really super time. Oh, look, here's another one. And another. There you go, bless you.'

Hugh   Well thank you very much indeed if you don't mind me saying so.

Stephen   I certainly don't mind you saying so, in fact it's very kind of you. Here's a fiver.

Hugh   Well, thank you I'm sure.

Stephen   Good. Well, I hope you're going to monitor the public's behaviour very closely Hugh, and if you find people approaching with five pound notes,

you'll come back on the programme and let
us know?

Hugh   I certainly will.

Stephen   Alright then. Just time now to go over to Devizes
and catch up with Chris and that giant sauna.

> VOX
> POP
>
> **Hugh**   They've got hotter pavements, I
> know that.

Tomorrow's World

Hugh   How many times have you walked out in front
of a bus, been knocked down and killed? Pretty
frustrating, isn't it?

Stephen Well, now there's a solution to that problem. A
company down in Truro in Cornwall have started
producing these lightweight travelling hats, which
can be folded very tightly indeed, but when
unpacked can be thrown away almost immediately.

Hugh   Which hopefully should eliminate that bus problem
at a stroke.

VOX
POP

Stephen That one with Trevor Howard
in it. And Celia Johnson.
That one. With a drop of
mayonnaise.

Spies Five

A park bench, in a television studio somewhere in Shepherd's Bush's famous London. Hugh approaches Stephen, who is sitting and feeding ducks from a brown paper bag.

Hugh   My cheque book is sometimes yellow.

Stephen   Yellow is the colour of some people's front porches.

Hugh   *(Slipping down next to Stephen)* Hello Control.

Stephen   Hello Murchison. Sorry to ask you to go through that coded exchange.

Hugh   Yes, it seemed rather odd, because we know each other quite well, don't we?

Stephen   That's a true thing to say, Tony, but the fact is we can't be too careful at the moment.

Hugh   Did you think perhaps that I might be a KGB man with a false head on?

Stephen   I hadn't entirely ruled it out.

Hugh   So.

Stephen   Mm. I expect you're wondering why we couldn't meet in my office, Tony.

Hugh   Not really, it's being redecorated, isn't it? I had a little peek through the door this morning when I was passing. I think I caught a glimpse of some rather attractive rolls of wallpaper. A sort of silvery stripe, with a textured bit.

Stephen   Yes. The cornice and moulding are going to be picked out in maroon.

Hugh	That sounds very adventurous.
Stephen	Mm. I find that makes a room look bigger. Well I've got to put my serious hat on now. Are you familiar with the term 'mole'?
Hugh	Surely a mole is an enemy agent planted deep within an organisation, such as ours, who pretends to be on one side but is really on the other all the time?
Stephen	Yes. They are beastly.
Hugh	Yes, very.
Stephen	Well, for some time, Murchison, the Minister and I have been ever so slightly anxious about the possibility of there being just such a 'mole' working inside our department.
Hugh	Oh lor.
Stephen	Yes. That's why I thought it would be more secure if we met here, not in my office.
Hugh	That's a smart and professional piece of thinking, Control.
Stephen	It's no good trying to be all private and secret if there's a mole listening to you all the time, probably laughing up his sleeve at you. If moles have sleeves.
Hugh	So a mole, with or without sleeves. Fff. In our department? That makes my blood boil.
Stephen	Mine too. It really is beginning to look like it. The Minister and I have decided to call the mole 'Duncan' by the way.
Hugh	Oh. Well I'm afraid that your theory about there being a mole may be wrong then, Control.
Stephen	I'm busy wondering why that should be, Tony?
Hugh	Well, we haven't got anyone called Duncan

228

working in the department. I could ask the computer to give information on people called Duncan until the cows come home, but it is such a quite common name. Especially in Scotland, I think.

Stephen   I may not have explained myself too well, Murchison. Duncan is just his code-name for the time being.

Hugh   What a devious business we're in, Control.

Stephen   Yes, I often think that it's a pity that we have to lie and conceal the truth so much. It leaves a not very pleasant taste in the mouth sometimes.

Hugh   Hear, hear.

Stephen   I have to say that I don't envy the mole, though.

Hugh   No, quite. I have to say that as well, Control. Because a mole has extra helpings of lying and concealing the truth to do.

Stephen   Yes. We've got quite enough on our plate just working for one country, haven't we, Tony?

Hugh   We jolly well have.

Stephen   If I had to do all my work twice I should get pretty fagged out. I shouldn't have a moment to call my own.

Hugh   Nor me.

Stephen   Bother him. Bother Duncan. Bother the Minister. Bother the whole damned lot of them.

Hugh   Yes. Mind you, it's given us an opportunity to get out into the fresh air for a change.

Stephen   That's true. And I expect the ducks will be pleased.

Hugh   They'd be jolly ungrateful if they weren't.

Stephen   Well I've got to have a small talk with the Minister now. Can I leave you to finish off feeding them?

Hugh   Certainly Control, leave the bag with me. You put the ducks out of your mind.

Stephen   Thanks Tony. Have done.

Hugh   B-bye, Control.

Stephen   B-bye, Murchison.

VOX
POP

Stephen   Sometimes I think they ought to build a ring road round the ring road. Ha ha. *(Laughs hysterically almost forever)*